'What Scott Elliot has done is provide a simple, clear and pleasantly sane beginner's guide to dowsing. He is not concerned with its history, or with science: only with showing how to learn to use a divining rod (or pendulum, or any of a number of alternative gadgets).' BRIAN INGLIS, *The Spectator*

'A comprehensive review of the whole subject written by a practical dowser of proven ability, it covers a wide field of experience over a number of years . . . I strongly recommend this book.'
Dr A. T. Westlake, *Radionic Medicine*, Vol. II, No. 12

'This very practical book should do much good to the cause of dowsing.' *British Society of Dowsers*, Vol. XXV, No. 176

Dowsing: One Man's Way

J. SCOTT ELLIOT

SPHERE BOOKS LIMITED
30/32 Gray's Inn Road, London WC1X 8JL

First published in Great Britain by Neville Spearman (Jersey) Ltd, 1977

Published by Sphere Books Ltd 1979

TRADE
MARK

Set in Monotype Baskerville

Printed in Great Britain by
William Collins Sons & Co Ltd
Glasgow

Acknowledgements

I am very grateful to all those who have assisted me with my Dowsing, to the very many who have helped me with excavations and to those involved in the production of this book.

J.S.E.

To Fay

Contents

Foreword.

The attitude towards dowsing is changing. A large number of people are interested in Extra Sensory Perception and dowsing as part of the ESP spectrum is accepted as a useful ability by many more people than was the case a short while ago. The generation that I belong to is sceptical and always asks for proof that dowsing works, whereas the young are open and prepared to have a try. Officialdom does not yet accept it, nor does Science although there are scientists in dowser's societies.

I feel that it is up to us to show that with accurate work by qualified dowsers it can be useful as a saver of time, labour and money in finding with accuracy many things underground and elsewhere, which at present can not be located by scientific instrument search.

It is with this in mind that I write this book for those interested in dowsing and its many applications.

I am often asked how I started dowsing and because it may encourage others to do likewise I tell the story for what it is worth.

I left the Army at the age of 54 and went to live in Dumfriesshire. There I quickly had all the work of a duty kind that I could manage, but there was something missing. Fortunately I started working in archaeology, assisted and indeed pressed by some very good friends. At the same time I happened to read a small book on Dowsing. Apart from knowing that there were a few people known as water diviners I knew nothing of the subject. The book interested me and I began to try out some of the exercises and found that it seemed to work for me. Thereafter followed 6 months hard labour teaching myself. Fortunately I met another retired soldier who had been a water finder for many years. He had started by finding half-crowns under the mess carpet on guest nights on the understanding that finding was keeping! He was able to help me from time to time with advice and I have always been grateful and very much indebted to him for his help and advice over the years.

The archaeology and the dowsing have since then gone hand in hand. Very soon I had the idea that I would be able to find unknown sites of value which did not show on the surface. The idea was that the professional archaeologists would then come and excavate them! I soon discovered that the professionals were not interested, partly because they did not believe in dowsing and also because they had more than enough sites of their own to get on with!

So my friends in our local society suggested that I learn to do the excavation myself. This I set about doing and I got to know well a number of professionals who instructed me as a novice worker on their sites and they have been valued and helpful friends ever since. That was the beginning.

PART I

SECTION I.

What is Dowsing. What can be done by Dowsing. Some basic rules. How does Dowsing work.

What is Dowsing.

My own, tentative definition of Dowsing is this:– "The ability to use a Natural Sensitivity which enables us to know things we cannot know by the use of the day to day brain or by learning, by experience, or by the use of the five physical senses."

It is, I believe, a matter of the Mind. I think there are very few objects that cannot be found by dowsing means and, in addition, there is much that can be found out by the use of the same means.

Dowsing enables us to work at any distance round the world and distance, depth or height seem to make no difference.

This ability has been, I believe, in man from the beginning. I suggest it helped him in early days to find his water, his food and his minerals. In addition it enabled him to know about and to communicate with the other sections of his tribe at a distance. There are still so-called primitive tribes in a few places who have these abilities to-day.

This natural sensitivity being much used in the early days was, in consequence, kept well developed. Then, as Man went on through the centuries, the ability was not needed so much and so tended to become atrophied.

In many religious sects through the ages this ability to 'know' was understood by the priesthood and often kept jealously guarded from the ordinary people. I think it is in the background of the original Christian teaching but it has got lost. I always think this is the explanation for the Oracle of

Delphi in its original state, a team of trained dowsers working on people's problems. Later, of course, it became corrupt and the double answer became the rule. But I do not believe that the Oracle could have started on a double answer basis, it must have produced good work to begin with.

The following tale was told me about the Oracle by a very eminent Greek scholar. There was a General who arrived with his army at the bank of a large river. He found his opponent was on the other side with his army. Being undecided as to what he should do he sent a runner off to Delphi with the message, 'If I cross the river with my army what will happen?' The reply came back. 'A great army will be destroyed.' So he was much cheered as he thought his was truly a great army. So he ordered his army over the river, but my nightfall his army was destroyed and he was a fugitive!

There is a lesson here for the modern dowser – it is essential to get the question framed correctly and this is not always easy.

In more recent centuries, western religions ostracised and preached against dowsing practices and particularly against so-called witchcraft with the result that they were suppressed and even made illegal, leading to further atrophy in man of this sensitivity through suppression and lack of use.

Nowadays there is a change in outlook. From being black, dowsing is slowly becoming at least white and, in places, it is even accepted though not as yet by officialdom nor by Science.

What can be done by Dowsing.

I believe there is very little in the physical world which cannot be found by dowsing and there is much in addition that can be found out. But I would emphasise two essentials here. To work effectively and with consistent success the dowser must first of all be properly skilled as a dowser. Secondly he must be knowledgeable and experienced in the particular fields in which he is working. Some fields need a lot of detailed background knowledge, and most fields need considerable experience.

I do not believe in the universal dowser. It is perfectly possible to have knowledge, experience and skill in several fields and it is also possible to start work in new fields, but the background has to be learnt and experience gained before consistently reliable results can be expected. Many of the failures experienced by dowsers are caused by venturing into new fields without sufficient knowledge and experience.

The following general list gives some idea of the many and varied fields to which dowsing can be applied. The list is by no means exhaustive.

Water. The location of underground streams at any depth, their line of flow and depth. Estimation of the quantity that can be extracted, and the quality of the water.

Minerals. Precious Stones. The location, demarkation and identification of the area, the line of the mineral lodes, depth and some estimate of quantity and quality.

Oil. Gas. The location of oil areas on land and under the sea, and the depth below surface. The estimation of comparative quantity and quality of the oil and the porosity of the strata in which the oil lies.

Archaeology. The location of unknown sites where nothing shows on the surface of the ground. The depth below surface of sites, the outline, the run of the defences, depth of ditches, the run of walls and buildings. Location of roads, grave sites and burials. The date of sites.

Location of sunk ships and submarines.

Building Sites. Examination for all purposes, the water runs under them, rock state, soil state, rock faults, old wells, cavities, cellars, drains, cables, etc.

Location of Cables, Pipes, Drains. The line of the run, depth. Location of fractures, leaks, blockages. Location of agricultural field drains.

Location of Tunnels and caves underground. The demarkation, size and depth of them.

Lost Articles.

Missing People. This is one of the most difficult tasks owing to the difficulty of identification. It should be approached with care, never lightly, and officially only after much practice.

Plant and Soil treatment. Mainly the improvement of the soil in relation to the plants or crops to be grown in it.
Medical. A number of qualified doctors and others use dowsing techniques to assist in diagnosis and in the selection of remedies.

Some Basic Rules

These are some basic rules which are a guide to beginners but apply at all stages of a dowser's career.

1. *Virtually all Dowsing is Seeking.* This must be appreciated and the mind focussed in this direction.
2. *Develop the Dowsing Sensitivity.* Before a dowser is any use he must develop the dowsing sensitivity. In order to do this he must learn the ability to cut out the brain and the five senses and allow the mind to reach out for the answer. He must practise this in his early training by exercises and in elementary dowsing work.
3. *Practice and Test on demonstrable Results.* To develop the sensitivity it is essential to practise and train on exercises and on work that has demonstrable results. If the results are not demonstrable the novice will never know if he is correct or not and hence in practice he may be using the brain or the imagination and not the mind.
4. *The Question asked must be Correct, Clear and Appropriate.* Surprisingly this is not always easy and care must be taken when framing the question. The wider one's dowsing interests the more I find this care in wording necessary.
5. *There must be a 'need' to know.* With a need to know the answer the Mind does seem to work with more precision. I think the reason why dowsers so often fail in tests set to them to demonstrate that dowsing works, is this element of the Need to Know. Under such test conditions there is seldom a need to know the answer, only a need to show that dowsing works – thus the mind machinery seems to get confused.
6. *Have Confidence that Dowsing works for you.* This is an

essential stage. Develop it and hang onto it, despite failures. So many people say to me, 'Oh it works for me. But I don't think I would be any good. I don't really trust it.' My reply to them is 'Oh ye of little faith.'

7. *It is essential to know the background of the field in which you are working*. Study it. There is no need to be an expert, but sufficient must be known to be able to understand the rudiments, general working, and language of the field. If the background is not known, stupid and unnecessary mistakes may occur and mistakes are costly.
8. *Be bold in application*. You have got to be prepared to take on things you have never tried before and which appear difficult. (This despite Rule 7 above. See Part III Case 15).
9. *Time*. If there is any question of Time in a dowsing problem this must be remembered and taken into account. If this is not done Remenance and other factors may lead to mistakes being made.
10. *Identification*. If there are many objects similar to the object sought there must be some form of identification in order to differentiate from others similar. Examples of this are humans and animals. If the object is well known to the dowser then the means of identification is not so necessary. The best identification is a blood spot, a hair or the combings of a brush, a fingerprint, photo or a piece of intimate garment belonging to and exclusively handled by the person. Hand writing is sometimes used, as are photographs, but I do not find these easy.
11. *Preconceived Ideas. Wishful Thinking*. These are the biggest menaces in dowsing. I believe they are the reason for the majority of dowsing failures among novices. Failure comes from one or other of these when the brain or one of the five senses is allowed to do the work and not the Mind. When this happens it is the Brain that activates the muscles that operate the tool in use instead of the Mind. All dowsers, however skilled, have to be aware of this and guard against mistakes from this cause.

How does Dowsing work

To be honest we don't know.

In the 1930's most people seemed to think that things emanated and that the dowser 'picked up' the emanations. So much was this thought that it was said that certain kinds of rods and pendulums had to be used for certain jobs. It was also thought that if, for instance, one was looking for Lead and carried a lead sample in the hand or the pocket, one was physically attracted to the lead vein. Ideas like this were current and believed.

This line of thought was, I believe largely the outcome of a very limited use of dowsing. Distant dowsing in its varied forms was hardly used and almost all dowsers worked only with water. Today when distant dowsing enables one to work in one's home on problems anywhere in the world and when great distance, great height or great depth seem to make no difference, some other explanation, other than just emanation has to be provided.

For myself I think there is a physical element in that the work starts in me, physical, and ends in the object sought which is also physical. But I believe the main part of the work is done by the Mind. I must explain the use of this word. I use the word Mind here in contradistinction to the Brain. The Brain as we know it, deals in the tangibles. A kind of computer which we train and feed all through life to remember, to reason, to appreciate situations, to store experience and to coordinate what the five physical senses, sight, smell, sound, touch, taste, tell us. The brain does much else beside, but it cannot do what the Mind can do.

The Mind, in the sense that I use it here deals with the intangibles, it covers those things commonly spoken of today as the super-conscious, the subconscious, the unconscious and the various other levels of consciousness and includes instinct and intuition. Very little is in fact known about these fields and most of us have our own words and our own ideas about them.

I classify the sensitivity used in dowsing as the product of this field and simplify it by calling it the Mind, but it does not matter what you call it so long as you recognise it as a sense or ability different from the day to day brain. Dowsing Sense or Intuition, as words, may be preferred by some.

I believe the trained and qualified dowser 'knows' the answer to his questions, in his mind. How this is done and how it works I do not know. One has to face up to the fact that most of the dowser's work is near miraculous in relation to present day knowledge and physical ability.

For myself I am prepared to accept this and get on with the work of using this ability for good and useful purposes. Personally, I do not believe we shall know how dowsing works until very much more is known about the workings of the Mind in general.

I have said that the dowser 'knows' the answer in his Mind. He can get at the answer simply by using the mind alone, but this is difficult and mistakes are easily made. So, to simplify the process of getting what is in the mind out into a simple visible or tangible signal he uses tools coupled with a code language of his own for the movement of the tools. These tools whatever they are, the hands alone, rods, pendulums, wands etc. are activated subconsciously by the muscles on the instructions of the mind and they move in accordance with the code language the dowser has arranged for himself. This is partly the explanation for the infinite number of variations in tools and tool movements used among dowsers.

SECTION 2

The Tools. Who can do it. How it is done.

The Tools

The first point to get clear about the tools is that there is no magic in any of them. They are inanimate indicators, moved subconsciously by the dowser himself in accordance with his own code language. I stress this as there have been, in the past, those who ascribe to the tools values that they do not possess.

Tools used by dowsers are many and various, but as this is a book mainly for beginners and largely about my own experience and way of working, I shall keep it as simple as possible and deal only with the simpler tools. Some dowsers use a number of differing pendulums and rods for carrying out different jobs. I would strongly advise beginners to keep it simple and make do with the minimum aids in their work.

Pendulums. These are merely weights suspended on the end of a line of some material. The weight can be made of any material and be of any size. Those used for outdoor work need to be larger and heavier than those used for indoor work so that they are not easily influenced by windy or wet weather. The shape is immaterial except that it must allow an easy, smooth swing, hence it is best to have a symmetrical shape and a fairly central or low centre of gravity.

Pendulums required for indoor work on maps and plans need a point of sorts at the bottom end. Also for this work it is best to have an opaque pendulum otherwise when working in artificial light with a transparent one an irritating light spot comes through and appears on the paper.

For suspension of the pendulum it is best to use an untwisted fibre. If a twisted fibre is used it tends to unwind and spin the pendulum in an irritating way. I use a plaited cord for outdoor work and nylon thread for indoor work.

The first pendulum I used was a very light, glass bauble off the top of a Christmas tree, about 1½ inches in diameter! This worked well in my learner stages and I recommend it as a learner tool for anyone who has difficulty at first in getting the heavier type of pendulum to work for him. But this one had no point on the bottom, and was of no use working on maps or plans, so it was discarded.

Since then I have used for indoor work a black plastic pendulum of the size and shape shown in the drawing. It weighs just under half an ounce. It will be noticed that the point at the bottom is not all that sharp, but in use on maps and plans I can work down to 1mm in distance with it and this is quite accurate enough for most of my work. There are many like these on the market and the dowser will chose the size and weight that suits him best. (See page 32.)

My pendulum is suspended on a piece of nylon about 2 inches in length. Some people like longer lengths but all dowsers must suit themselves. For map dowsing a short length of suspension is preferable for accuracy and speed in working.

Normally I do not use a pendulum for outdoor work, but there is the odd occasion when there is not room in which to use a rod and on these occasions I do. When this is so I use a wooden pendulum which is in fact the knob which used to hang at the end of the cord for pulling a curtain across a window! Hung on a plaited cord 5 inches long, it works well for me.

Angle Rods. The simplest form of angle rod is a piece of heavy fence wire or other metal bent to form a long arm and a short arm as shown below. The weight and length of each arm is to the dowser's taste. But it is as well not to have the rods too light as they are then difficult to use in bad weather.

Most dowsers use two of these rods, one in each hand, but I know of one good water finder who uses only one. There are some rods on the market with the holding end enclosed in a holder which is gripped in the hand within which the rod is free to turn at will. I think these may be very difficult to use in bad weather, and when moving over rough ground.

I seldom use angle rods nowadays, but did use them in the early days and I find that most people find them easier to operate when first learning. The ones I use are made of heavy fence wire 3/16th inch in diameter, the long arm is 18 inches long and the short arm 6 inches. This for some might be too big and heavy, but as much of my work was done in all weathers and often in windy and hilly places the weight was necessary.

V Rods. There are various types and sizes of V rods. The governing factor is that the rod is springy and can be held under tension. They can be made of a variety of materials, the most popular are Wood, Whalebone and Nylon. (see Frontispiece Plate I).

The traditional V rod is the Hazel fork, but apple is popular too. It does not matter much what wood is used as long as it is springy and firm and the two arms approximately the same thickness. But wood is not used much nowadays and it is not recommended. The trouble is that it tends to dry quickly and then breaks easily. The loss or breakage of a rod when doing a job of work can be serious and is always a nuisance.

Whalebone. Because wooden rods tended to break easily, many dowsers of 20 years ago changed to whalebone and this has been a popular material. It also tends to get dry and may break and in addition it is no longer easy to get other than in short lengths.

The V rod is made by tying two lengths of whalebone together at one end. The tie must be made firmly. The section of the whalebone can be flat or circular and the length as required. The length of such rods vary from about 24 inches in length to finger rods only about 5 inches long.

I have used whalebone for a number of years. My own rod is circular in section, slightly under 1/8th inch in diameter. It is

18 inches long with the end 1½ inches involved in the tie up. I gravitated to this length from a 12 inch one, simply because I was told by someone long ago that I would be more sensitive with the longer rod. I think this is probably rubbish, but I am now used to this length and have adhered to it, despite the disadvantage of a long rod that is difficult to pocket or carry when not in use. It is a good example of a shibboleth, to which I refer in Section 5, one of those things we are told are important which we adopt, then find they don't matter, but by then we are stuck with them!

Nylon. Because whalebone is not easy to get and because it does break if allowed to dry out too much, the modern material to use is Nylon, provided the correct weight and dimensions for the dowser's own tastes can be obtained. The two advantages of using nylon are that it will not break and secondly a white rod can be used. I find that for one reason or another one is apt to lay the rod down on the ground quite often and later it is hard to find if the colour is black whereas the white is easy to see against most backgrounds.

When making the rod from two lengths of circular plastic it is as well to cut and shape the ends to be tied, so that two flat surfaces lie snugly together, making the tie much firmer.

I have a white plastic rod of circular section 3/16 of an inch in diameter. It is 18 inches long overall, with 1½ inches of the length involved in the tie at the end. For those used to a rather stiff whalebone rod it might be a bit 'soft' to handle at first but I find it satisfactory to use, easy to find if I lay it down for any reason and above all things it is virtually indestructable.

In southern Libya, on the northern edge of the Sahara some years ago while there on an excavation I had a whalebone rod with me and for quite a lot of the day when it was not in use it lay on the ledge just inside the windscreen of the Land Rover, in the full sun. Some days later it broke in my hand while in use. I usually have a spare rod with me, but this time I had none. The only trees were a few date palms and useless for my purpose. Fortunately after some time I found some very rusty pieces of wire which I cut and fashioned into angle rods and so was able to go on with the work. The moral of this tale is, always have a spare tool handy and use tools that are reasonably unbreakable.

Wands. I use this name because it is used by some and it is descriptive.

The wand was a 3 foot long, narrow piece of springy wood, perhaps a piece of a thin branch. Today it is made of Nylon about $\frac{1}{4}$ inch diameter and still 3 foot long. They are not common tools, but some dowsers use nothing else and for some of us they have special uses which will be explained in the next section.

The Rubber Stick Pad. I must mention the rubber stick pad. I do not use it myself but some dowsers do and in particular it is used by those practising Radionics. It consists simply of a small area of sheet rubber stretched over a frame which is fixed and will not move when being used. The operator searching a map, or say a list, has in mind the question to be answered, passes a finger of one hand lightly over the rubber at rapid intervals while operating a pointer with the other hand. Until the key area on the map or list is indicated by the pointer the finger moves easily over the rubber. But when the key area or the key word is reached the finger feels the rubber go sticky.

What happens of course is that the mind working on the problem 'knows' when the key area or word is reached and operates the finger on the rubber so that stick is achieved, probably by using more pressure.

I find this system a complicated way of doing things and prefer to use a pendulum directly over the map or the list of words. It is a much more direct and simple method and does not involve trying to do two things at the same time in different directions! There is also a potential area of error too, for unless the pointing movement is kept accurately in time with the finger touching the rubber, it may pass over an area when the finger is not in contact and so that area may be missed. I mention this only for the benefit of beginners who I believe should keep their work as simple as possible.

Hands Alone. This will be explained in Section 3. Using the tools.

Who can do it.

Let us clear up one point straight away. Qualified dowsers are not 'odd' people. They are very ordinary men and women who have developed their sensitivity for practical purposes and use it on practical problems the outcome of which are demonstrable, thus their work can be seen to be correct or not.

From experience in testing and in trying to help people I would say that somewhere about 10% of people could be good dowsers. Of the remainder I am sure many could be average dowsers if they wanted to be and if they were able to find a suitable use they could practice and train on. Both these conditions are absolutely essential for success for all novices. The latter can be quite a problem sometimes but must be overcome and will be if the novice is keen enough.

There are many people who are quite keen and interested, but who have never found a use for their ability so have never properly developed their sensitivity. It is from the ranks of these untrained semi-sensitives that, I am sorry to say, much of the harm to the reputation of dowsing comes, for although untrained and unpracticed they take on jobs and fail and so bring dowsing into disrepute. I say to these folk, either go on, find an outlet, practice and train seriously, or put away the pendulums and the rods and just remain interested.

How it is done and my own way of Working.

I well remember at the end of a lecture when I had talked about my dowsing in some detail and given instances of success and failure and had tried to give reasons for the failure a lady came up to me and said, 'Oh but you did not tell us how you do it!'

It is extremely difficult to describe in sufficient detail how one does the simplest of things like walking down stairs, or how one hits a ball with a racquet when it is moving across to one's left, with the racquet held in the right hand, or even how to kick a football accurately so that it goes into the top right hand corner of the goal! These are comparatively simple physical actions, but it is very much more difficult to describe a combined Mind and Physical feat where the simple mechanisms of it are just not understood and indeed not even accepted as possible by many people!

However I seem able to get it across verbally to pupils, so here goes. What follows is necessarily my own way but it is similar to that used by a number of practising dowsers. I am sure there are other good ways so if mine does not suit you try one of the others!

The approach I describe is basically the same whatever the tool I am using and whatever the method being used for the particular problem whether it be distant dowsing, map dowsing or ground dowsing.

I think it is because I am naturally somewhat phlegmatic but my approach to dowsing is careful and quiet. I do not get violent movement of the rod or pendulum, nor do I get ill effects when working over water, oil or minerals as some dowsers say they do. I do not get tingles in my fingers, my toes, or up my back, nor do I get unduly tired. All this may sound pretty dull but I think it is the way I want it to be, thus it works for me this way

When I have a dowsing problem to solve the procedure divides itself basically into two main parts. The first is the straight forward study of the problem and the factors. This I call the Brain appreciation. The second part is the actual dowsing work which must be done by the Mind (or whatever you like to call it, the subconscious or intuition or whatever) and not by the brain.

The second part the actual dowsing divides itself into three parts, but I come to that later.

The Brain appreciation.

1. Get all the information available that has a bearing on the

problem. Sum it up. Get associated with it and allow yourself to get thoroughly soaked up in the problem.

2. Decide how you are going to set about solving the problem.

3. Get clear the sort of questions that will have to be answered by the dowsing.

4. Decide the correct form of the first question to be asked.

5. *Then pause and relax.*

The Dowsing.

6. When ready with the tool in the hand get the first question clear in the Mind. Visualise the Object sought as clearly as possible.

7. Shut the brain away from the dowsing problem and allow the Mind to feel out for the answer to the question. Start moving the tool – Seeking.

8. Keep moving and keep the object sought clearly in mind. Be neutral as to the results. Be relaxed.

9. Once mentally locked onto the object of search I do not have to 'concentrate' but the Object is clearly in mind.

10. The novice may like to think of the tool as a 'feeler' or whatever expression is preferred.

11. Expect the tool to 'encounter' what you seek as you move it and expect it to respond to the object in accordance with your own code language. Expect it to start responding a short while before arriving at the location of the object.

12. When you feel the tool beginning to respond, slow down your movement and approach the location of the object with caution so that the final indicated position is plotted exactly.

All this may sound fanciful, difficult, complicated, or it may sound unduly simple, but the fact is that when the 'drill' is known, it all becomes automatic and there is no difficulty.

The nub of the matter really lies in three things:-

Getting the question right.

Being clear in the Mind as to the object sought.

Being able to use the Mind and let it feel out for and respond to the object of search. To enable this to happen the dowser must be Neutral in outlook while using his tools and he must Not allow the Brain to try to do the work!

Once the novice has mastered these three things he is well on the way towards teaching himself to be a dowser.

My Dowsing Stages. Most of my work is in archaeology but the stages described below apply to many types of work and usually there are three stages.

Stage 1. This is done preferably at home. This is distant dowsing work done on a map or plan or by question and answer. The bulk of the work on a problem is done at this stage and most of the detail. If necessary large areas can be covered on maps or by question and answer, but on the other hand great detail can be achieved, usually much more than would ever be possible when working 'on the ground'.

Stage 2. Is on the ground and is to check and confirm the accuracy of the stage 1 results. This is a necessary stage and one I do not like having to omit. Odd things can happen as I found long ago when I thought I had found by Map Dowsing a nice rectangular archaeological site, it was in the right sort of position too according to the map. When I went to do the Stage 2 work I found there was a small town reservoir there just the size and shape I had picked up in my map dowsing! Stage 2 also enables one to mark accurately the position and outline of what one is seeking. If this is not done by the dowser in person on the spot, mistakes of all sorts can happen when excavation or drilling take place later.

Stage 3. Is the stage of Proof. In archaeological work it involves an excavation however small, to demonstrate that the dowsing is correct and that what was suspected from the dowsing results is in fact there. No dowsing job of any sort is of any real worth until this third proof stage has been successfully carried out.

In many cases it means waiting months or even years before the proof stage can be carried out and dowsers often have to be patient.

There are occasions when either Stage 1 or Stage 2 can be, or have to be omitted for one reason or another but not Stage 3, that is the vital one. I do not like omitting any stage but sometimes circumstances make it necessary.

For examples of all three stages being used see Part 3. Case 4 Swinbrook. Case 11 Chieveley Manor. For an example of omission of Stage 2 see Case 12 The Keys.

SECTION 3.

Using the Tools. Counting, part of the Code Language.

Using the Tools.

Most of what follows in this section must inevitably be based on my own way of working but there are other ways and I do not imply that my way is the one that novices must follow. I put it forward as a way that is simple and that works.

I have said before that dowsers are highly individualistic in their ways and methods of working and that this really stems from the fact that they are using a means we do not fully understand which is based on the Mind.

The tools are used so that what is 'known' in the Mind by the dowser can be brought out and recognised by the use of one of the five physical senses, Taste, Touch, Sight, Sound and Smell. The senses usually used are those of sight and touch in that the tools move visibly and tangibly in a certain way in accordance with the dowser's own code language of tool movements. This code language is built up by the dowser gradually as he progresses, part being what he learns from others and part being his own invention.

The sense of touch alone can be used for certain purposes by some. It is possible to run a finger over a map searching for something and know by the feel when the finger is over the correct spot. In my case the finger seems to stop sliding easily over the map and tends to get 'sticky' at the point sought. This method is possible for linear and area subjects but it cannot be very accurate as the finger is too large for pinpoint accuracy. I find it useful sometimes for getting a general impression or a quick check. When I do use this method I use the tip of the second finger of the left hand. As I use the pendulum in the left hand it is probably instinctive to use a finger of the same hand.

It would be true to say I also use the sense of touch when using the pendulum and the rods, in that as I get close to the object of search I can feel the tools beginning to respond a short way before I arrive at the object and by the type of movement and the feel, I know that I am getting near. These are movements I can both feel and see so it would be true to say that I am using both the sense of sight and touch.

Some dowsers say they get a sense of taste over certain subjects. In my early days I used to get an unpleasant taste in my mouth when finding water but I discarded this as it did not seem to help accurate location and was a bit of a nuisance! I think I had only developed it because I read in one of the books that someone had had this experience, so you are warned! It is a good example of a Shibboleth. Fortunately I was able to discard this one. Evelyn Penrose has stated that she used to feel ill over Oil when searching for it. The moral is – Try not to adopt shibboleths if you can avoid them. Some dowsers have talked of using the sense of smell. Witch doctors in Africa and other places have for long talked of 'smelling out' the object of their search. Whether this is just expressive of the way of searching using a natural and understood animal hunting simile, or whether they actually think they use a sense of smell I do not know. But whatever the use of the other senses the ones most commonly used are those of touch and sight.

Whatever the dowsing problem, whatever the tool being used, whatever the distance of the object, its depth or height, I find my dowsing feelings are exactly the same, only the methods vary.

Before starting to operate the tool I have a clear question in my Mind. I have switched off the brain from the particular problem and have alerted the Mind (or dowsing sense or intuition or whatever you like to call it) to feel out and provide the answer. The above action is presumed all through this section and is mentioned here to avoid undue repetition.

Pendulums

I very seldom use a pendulum out of doors, but when I do the methods, movements and the code language used are exactly the same as for the pendulum indoors. The following therefore applies to both uses, although it describes mainly indoor work.

I hold it in my left hand and this is an advantage as it leaves my right hand free to hold a pencil for map marking or any writing necessary without having to disturb the pendulum hand (Plate III). Many other people of course use the right hand.

The indoor pendulum is hung on a two inch long piece of nylon. The outdoor one on a five inch long plaited cord. I have a knot tied where I like to hold so that it does not slip through the finger hold.

Some people like the pendulum tied on a long length of line, this makes for slow pendulum action and not such accurate

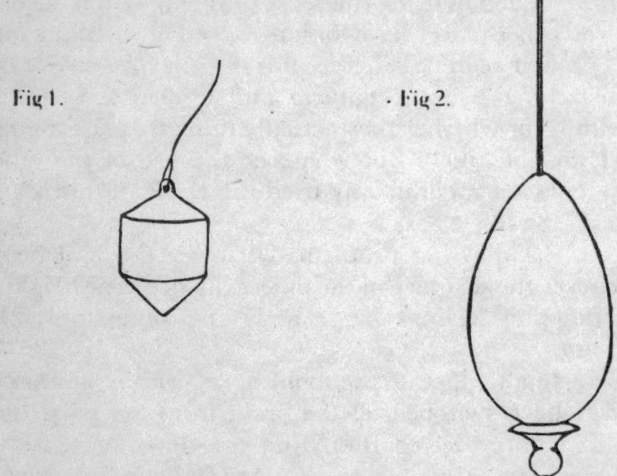

Fig 1. My indoor pendulum half size.
Fig 2. My outdoor pendulum half size.

18

centreing when trying to plot a point. My work requires a quick Yes or No, or a quickly located exact spot on a map or plan, or a quick count to arrive at a depth or age or date etc. For this sort of work a short tied pendulum gives very much quicker results and is far less laborious to use.

The body position when seated working at a table is important, particularly for novices, so I stress it here. A slovenly position or an awkward position can lead to slovenly inaccurate work, in part because the mind process follows suit and partly because the accuracy of the pendulum work is affected. The exact centering of the pendulum on the map is essential for map dowsing and for this one needs the part of the map being worked on close in front of one. If attempts are made to work at the far edge at a distance it is very difficult to get the centering and the marking accurate. For the novice I suggest sitting upright and close to the table with the map plan or object to be worked on just in front of the body. I like a hard surface to work on so always have a piece of hardboard on which things lie. The pendulum is held between the

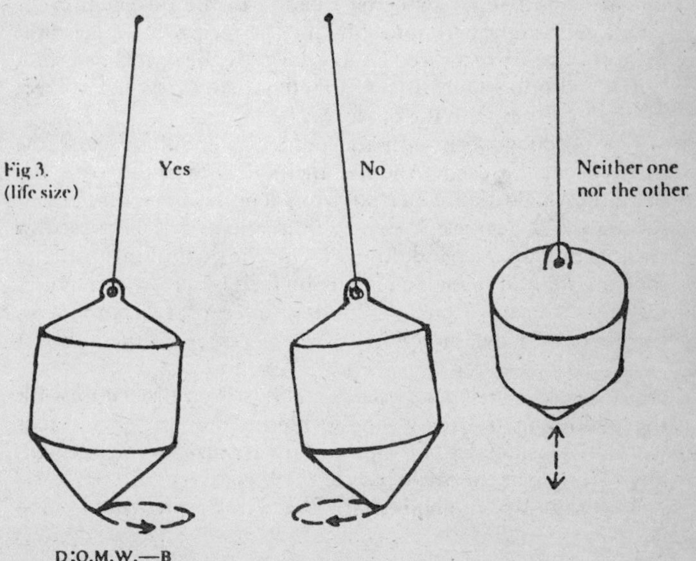

Fig 3.
(life size)

forefinger and thumb, forearm parallel to the table and elbow off the table. The position should be relaxed. The other hand can steady papers or maps being worked with and at the same time bring the dowser into mental contact with whatever he is working on, it can as well hold a pencil if that is needed.

Yes. Is an anti clockwise circular swing or gyration.

No. Is a clockwise circular swing or gyration. These are the main movements in ordinary question and answer work but there is another that I use and that is an oscillating movement towards me and from me. This means either 'I don't know' and is associated with a badly phrased question or 'neither one thing nor the other', e.g. Question 'Is this food good for me?' It would mean 'It will neither do good nor harm'.

Direction finding. First think of what is to be found. The question can then be phrased as 'In what direction is X?' When working indoors on a map allow the pendulum to swing and it should settle swinging steadily in the direction of X. Don't get caught here into thinking the reciprocal is the right answer. The correct direction is known by the swing, as I said, but in addition there is a distinct pull towards the correct direction rather than the other way.

For outdoor work with the outdoor pendulum the same method can be used. Another method is to stand with the pendulum held out at partial arm's length, then pivot round through 360 degrees. When the direction of X is passed, a distinct pull on the pendulum is felt as the pendulum wishes to indicate that direction and centre on it. It is best to swing back through the 'pull' position quietly once or twice to make certain of the exact direction.

Search Procedure with the Pendulum. This search procedure with the pendulum is equally applicable for indoor and outdoor work. The principles of the procedure are also applicable with any tool such as the angle rods or the V rod.

There are two methods that I use. The first is what I call a

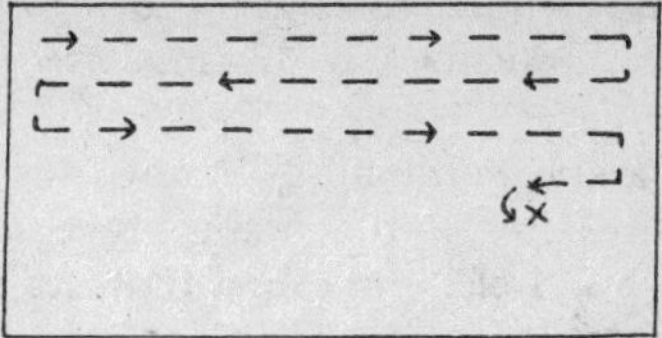

Fig 4. Detailed area search. The distance between search lines is about one inch but varies with the size of the object sought.

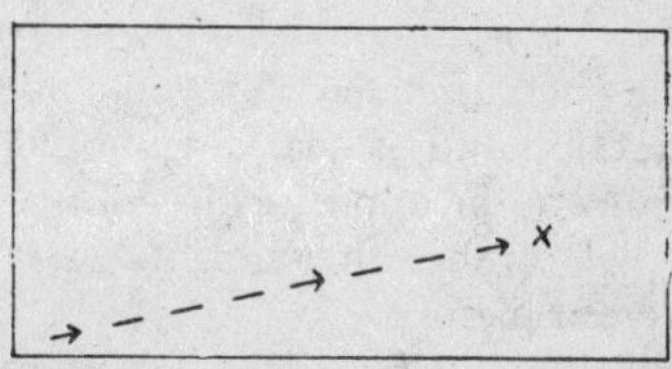

Fig 5. Directional and Distance Search.

Detailed Area Search and the other a Directional and Distance search. In the detailed area search I move the pendulum, hanging steady on its line, systematically over the area to be searched having in mind clearly the object of the search. When the pendulum gets over or near the object it will try to centre on it and try to pull towards it. Thus if I go beyond or to one side I will get the feeling that it is pulling back towards the key point where the object of the search lies. When the pendulum centres accurately the object of the search should be there directly under it so I lower it carefully to the paper and mark the spot with a dot.

In the other method, the directional and distance search, I start with the pendulum outside the area of search and get the appropriate question clearly in mind. Perhaps it might be 'Where Is X'. The pendulum will then start to swing, or oscillate towards the direction of X. I move it gently in the direction of swing and follow the direction of its pointing and it will continue to swing until it is over the near edge of what is sought, X, when it will try to centre. I lower it carefully to the spot it centres on and mark it. In this case we will call this point A.

Having found one point on X I now wish to outline it. Whether it is linear or rounded the procedure is the same though the operation of the method requires modification to suit the shape of the object.

Fig 6(a) shows the line of approach to A. By the same sort of approach find another point on the edge of X to the right or left of A. (Fig 6(b)). Continue to approach the line of X at points further to the right and mark where the pendulum centres with a dot each time. See that you come at X from the same general direction and as near at right angles as you can. Do not come at it from the opposite direction at this stage as if you do you will pick up the other side of X if it has width and that will confuse your picture.

By now you will have the feel of the pendulum reaction to X so there is no need to let it swing towards X. I usually keep it still and move it up towards the line of X and when I get to the line I feel the pendulum wanting to centre on and swing along the line of X. You will see by the direction of the arrows in Fig 6(c) that you have to vary the line of approach if X is not a straight line. As you do not know where changes will occur you will sometimes make the approach from a rather narrow angle, this does not matter as long as you are careful to get the centreing point accurately marked.

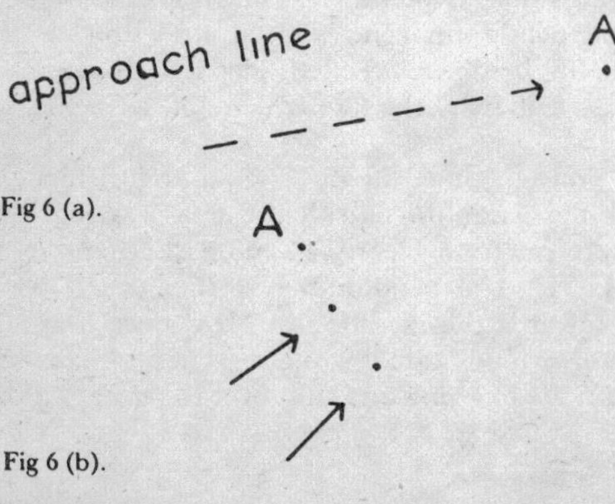

Fig 6 (a).

Fig 6 (b).

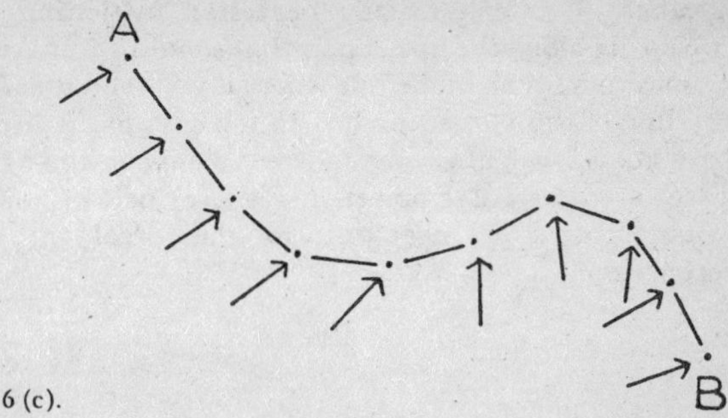

Fig 6 (c).

Having got the line of X from A to B next see if it has width. To do this approach from the opposite direction thinking of 'The other side of X' or whatever is appropriate. If you are skilled enough you can start from the already found side of X and work from there outwards, but if the width is narrow it may not be easy.

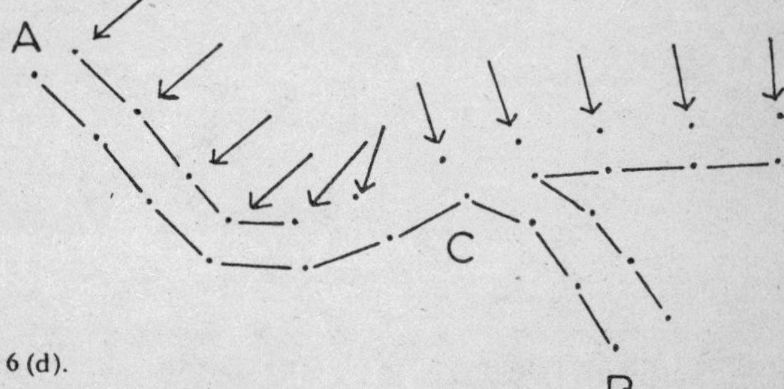

Fig 6 (d).

You will see (Fig 6(d)) that starting from A all goes well till we get to C. Here you pick up an unexpected part of X. If X was a stream this might be a tributary, or if working with a track it might be a track junction. I mention this as practical problems of this sort arise often.

After marking all the dowsed points I usually join them up to show they are connected and also to get a picture of what the object looks like. Be careful to join up only the ones related to each other. This can usually be tested by letting the pendulum swing along the line of points, it should swing freely until it comes to a break in the line where it will tend to swing across the line of the plotted points. In the case of Fig 6(d) I would have got a break at C where there is a change and again in the case of the circular object in Fig 6(e) below, at C I would have got a change due to the break in the circumference.

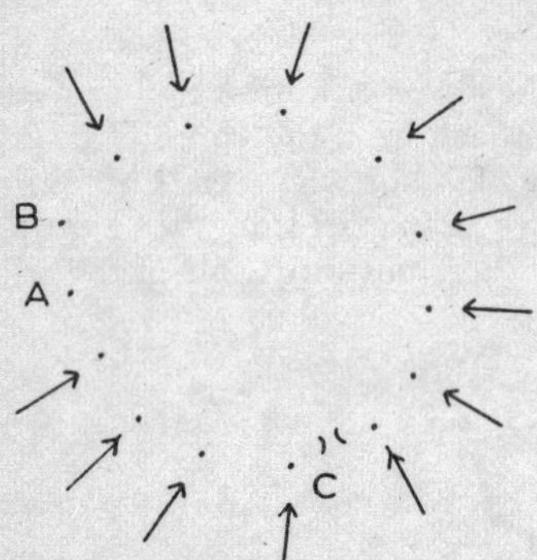

Fig 6 (e).

If dealing with a circular type of object I start the same way as for a linear and find the first three points. The line of approach of the pendulum will have to be changed considerably each time so that the right angle approach can be made when working round from A to B.

Having got the outside of the object now test to see if the outside edge has width. To do this, either work from the outside line inwards, which may be difficult, or work from the centre out towards the outside line, thinking of the inside edge of what has been found. (Fig 6 (f)).

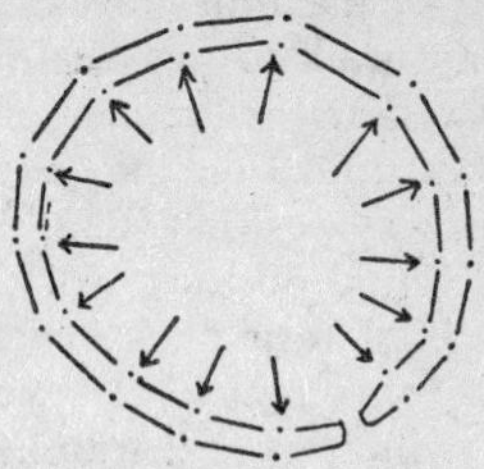

Fig 6 (f).

The Angle Rods

These are usually used for any dowsing work other than on maps. Personally I seldom use them nowadays as I find the V rod easier to handle in all types of country and in all weathers, but this is a purely personal preference. Most beginners find that the angle rod is the easiest type of rod to start with and so I usually start pupils off with the angle rods for outdoor work.

The Start Position (see Plate II) as I call it is with a rod held in each hand (some dowsers use only one). The short end is held in the fist with the long ends pointing forward and parallel to each other, the rods being comfortably balanced in the hands. Each forearm parallel to the ground, upper arms hanging straight down relaxed and elbows not drawn in to the body.

Move then towards the object of search, keeping the rods held steady in the hand and with the question clearly in the background of the mind. With a clear question the operator should only react to what is sought and to nothing else.

When I am getting close to the object sought the forward ends of the rods start moving in towards each other, then cross and continue to move over each other until they lie parallel to each other across the front of the body. When they arrive in this position I know I am directly over the object sought.

I call this position of the rods the 'Found Position'. (Plate IV). When the ends of the rods start moving towards each other I slow down my walk so that the final Found Position can be accurately placed on the ground.

Novices may at first find that the rods may not do more than cross in the half way position (Plate V) but this does not matter and the full found position will come with practice. Most novices are a bit late in their reactions and therefore tend to mark the object sought a bit beyond where in fact it really is. This fault will emerge if training is carried out on objects the position of which can be accurately demonstrated. I cannot emphasise too strongly the need to train and practise over objects the true position of which is demonstrable.

There is a variant in rod movement for some people, with them the rods tend to move outwards instead of inwards.

Direction Finding. For this I use one rod held lightly in the fist, arm extended. I have clearly in mind what I seek and wish to know the direction in which it lies. I then swing slowly on my own axis. As I swing, the rod will react to the required direction by tending to point to it as I continue to swing. So I swing back and allow it to centre on a direction. It may be necessary to swing once or twice across the apparent direction in order to get it correct.

Distance Finding. For this I use two rods. Having got the direction I then visualise what I seek and the appropriate direction and start counting in feet, or yards etc. When nearing the key distance in my counting the rods will tend to move and be in the found position at the key distance.

The Yes and the No. I do not like to use the angle rods for finding an answer which is simply Yes or No. I prefer to do it by other means. If I did I would use the start position for No and the found position for Yes.

Following a Line. The angle rods can be useful for following a line. This can be a line on the surface of the ground such as the

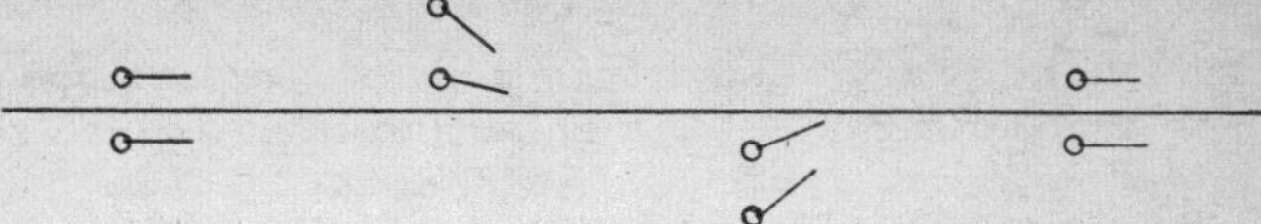
Fig 7. Following a line.

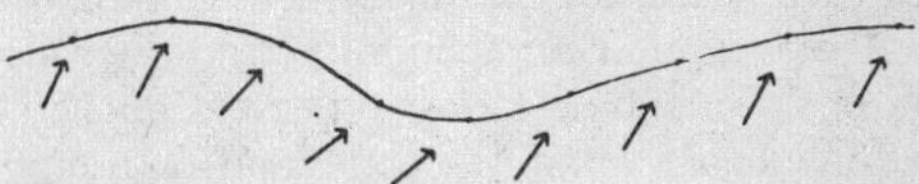
Fig 8. Plotting a line.

'scent' left by a person or an animal or it can be the line underground of an object.

First find the line by dowsing then turn on to the direction of run and start following with the rods in the search position. If you get to the right of the line the rods will swing to the left as if pointing to the line, if you get too much to the left the rods will swing right and point towards the line. By this means, and with practice a person or an animal can be followed without much difficulty.

As I said, this method can be used for tracing the line of objects underground too. Much depends on the circumstances and what is required but the alternative is to find and peg the line of the object at intervals, marking the near edge. This is a more accurate method for finding the actual position of the line and whether this or the other method is used will depend on the object of the exercise.

Unless actually following a surface 'scent' where the exact position of the line does not matter so much, I prefer to use the alternative as by this method the exact position of the line can be found.

When using this method, whatever the tool being used, it is as well to come at the object at an angle so that the position of the pegs marking the previous plotted positions cannot be seen as there is a risk of being influenced mentally by them.

The V Rods.

Beginners often find the holding of the V rod difficult mainly because it feels unnatural and strained. The two most common holds are described below, but there are a variety of others.

For the normal fairly long rod the hold is shown in Plate I Frontispiece. Here the ends of the rod are held between the thumb and the base of the forefinger, with the palm upwards and the fingers wrapped comfortably round the rod to steady it. The rod position should be at 45 degrees above horizontal and it should be held so that it is under tension but still able to rotate in the hand. For beginners a light hold is desirable.

The forearm is parallel to the ground, upper arm vertical and the shoulders and arms relaxed. This I call the 'Search Position'.

When the dowser on the move gets close to the position over the object sought, the rod starts to move slowly in the hand and the tip starts to go down. With me the rod will be pointing straight down when I am directly over the object sought. In fact from experience I know it ought to be directly below the ball of my big toe! This is my 'Found Position'. (see Plate VI). For some dowsers the rod turns up instead of down. I was once showing two policemen how to use the V rod. One man was large and beefy and the other very slim. I gave them each a rod and explained to them how to use it. I told them there was a 1 inch water pipe running under the lawn somewhere in front of them and I explained about visualising what they sought. They then set off down the lawn side by side and after about a dozen paces the rod in the hands of the large beefy one turned down sharply while the rod in the hands of the slim one turned up with a snap and hit him on the chest and they were just about correct as regards the location of the pipe. They were two very surprised policemen! It should not be thought from this that there is any connection between the rod movement and the weight of the operator! It is I suppose to do with the way the rod is held. For me the only time the rod comes up instead of down is when I am over a cavity of some sort, natural or artificial, but this is simply part of my own code of rod movement.

The other hold is used with very short rods, this is usually described as the finger hold. The arms of the small V rod are held between the tips of the forefinger and thumb with the rod pointing upwards at an angle of 45 degrees. The rod is held at about the level of the chest. On approaching the object sought the tip of the rod tends to move downwards and over the object it is pointing straight down.

For myself when using a V rod I always keep my eyes on the tip of the rod so when I get close to the object I can see and feel it start to move. I think this habit helps to keep my Mind concentrated on the job and helps to prevent my attention being distracted by other things.

The novice may find that at first he is easily distracted and has to concentrate unduly to get accurate results but after a while this phase passes with practice and he is able to work in a more relaxed way even with people about him and does not have to concentrate so hard. It is as well in the beginning to try to avoid working among distractions as they do not help. Once confidence is achieved and experience is gained, distractions can be shut out, if they cannot be avoided. Personally I much prefer working quietly on my own or with one quiet helper to carry things. Don't use a chatterer!

Nowadays I can work quite happily among a lot of people getting on with their own business, they must do this and not interfere with me. I once had to work on a building site in the middle of Kidderminster where they had pulled down and removed all visible signs of buildings over a large area which was then covered with piles of gravel, piles of wood, Bulldozers and so on. I was trying to confirm the position of some wells which I had map dowsed at the request of the building firm who knew of their possible existence and were anxious to avoid building over one without knowing of its position. (Part III. Case 10). I was happily dowsing among the turmoil of the site once I had got used to it, but one day I was working close to the temporary fence surrounding the site. Outside the fence were many people going about their business and I paid no attention at all until I felt strongly that someone was bothering me. I looked up and saw a man in a hat and rain coat gazing at me. I paid no attention and went on with my work but found that the man still seemed to interfere with my feelings. I tried to continue paying no attention but it was no use and shortly I gave up and went to work elsewhere. This is the only time that this sort of interference has happened to me.

Direction Finding. With the V rod in the search position, the object clearly in mind, I swing on my axis with the Mind searching. When I feel a small pull down on the rod I continue the swing for a little bit then with the rod still in the search position I swing back past the position where I got the pull. If I get this pull again I know that it is probably the direction that I want. I may test this again once or twice. When I talk of a pull on the rod it is really like a small movement of the rod in the hand but it does remind me of the feeling one gets fishing when a fish touches the fly or lure but does not take it.

Distance Finding. With the V rod in the search position and facing in the direction of the object to which the distance is required, I keep the object clearly in mind and start counting in the appropriate measure. In time with the counting I tap my heel on the ground, this is to help to overcome the initial inertia of the rod in my hand. When I get near to the key figure the tip of the rod tends to move downwards until I have counted the correct distance when the rod will be in the found position.

Following a Line. Following a line with this tool is not as easy as with the angle rods. I can do it slowly for a short distance by holding the rod in the search position, I find the line in one place and swing on to it, then move along it. As I move along it I 'feel' it by moving the rod from right to left across the body about every other pace. Each time the rod crosses over the line I feel the rod move in the hand and I adjust my direction accordingly. It is only possible to do this with any accuracy over short distances and it is a slow method. Personally I prefer the method described when using the angle rods, which consists in coming up to the line at intervals and establishing its exact position. (Fig 8).

The Yes and the No. I do not like to use the V rod for finding an answer which is simply Yes or No. I prefer to use other means, but if I have to use the rod I pose the question then start the heel tapping to help to overcome the initial inertia of the rod. If the rod does not move the answer is No but if it moves to the found position the answer is Yes.

The Wand.

This is a tool which very few dowsers use today, but I find it useful for certain purposes so include it here.

Those who use it normally carry it by one end pointing downwards at an angle of about 45 degrees. Having got the question clear start walking towards the object of search. When the forward end of the wand comes over the object it will react in the way the operator requires in accordance with his code. The one I use is a straight up and down motion of the wand end. Others use a gyration movement of the wand end. It is a useful tool for following a line as the forward tip will tend to point back towards the line if one moves too far right or left.

It can be used for counting in all its forms and for Yes and No, I use the same gyrations as for the pendulum, that is to say anti clockwise is Yes and clockwise is No.

Normally I only use it for searching places that are out of my reach with the other tools either perpendicularly or horizontally. Instances of these are parts of walls above my head, something the other side of a gap I cannot cross, or the sides and bottoms of ditches which for some reason I cannot get into.

There is one good water finder I know who uses a wand type of tool which he holds centrally with the arm straight down from the shoulder in the 'trail' position, to use a military expression. I do not know his code signals but he has a full range for his work.

The Hands Alone.

(Plate VII & VIII).

There are occasions when it is extremely useful to be able to use the hands alone with no other tool. These are when it is not possible to use one of the conventional tools, or sometimes when it is undesirable to do so. There are also occasions when a tool has been lost or left behind so I would strongly recommend beginners to start using their hands alone fairly early in their training. It can be as accurate a method as any other but having said that I must admit that I prefer to use one of the tools for real accuracy.

Not long ago I was doing a dowsing study of certain things to do with Churches and Cathedrals and most of the work was done by distant dowsing but confirmation had to be obtained 'on the ground'. It is just not feasible to wander round a Cathedral with a rod among the many visitors that are already in the building when one gets there, so an ability to use the hands alone was useful.

I know of three methods used by different dowsers and beginners can find out for themselves if any of these suit them and if not find their own.

Method (a). Hold the hands out, palms down, forearm parallel to the ground, upper arm hanging straight down, relaxed. This is the search position. Move towards the object of search, do not look at the hands, be relaxed. When the object is near the hands tend to rise. When over the object the hands will be about four inches higher than in the start position. Then as you move past the object the hands will drop and shortly return to the start position.

Method (b). This procedure is the same as in the above method except that the hands drop on approaching the object and rise again to the search position when past it.

Method (c). This is my own. I was shown method (a) but was never able to do it so found my own way and pass it on. In the start position the hands are held in front of the body in a very relaxed position with the palms facing each other and about 16 inches apart. The forearms horizontal and the upper arms hanging straight down, shoulders and arms completely relaxed. Before starting towards the object of search I am clear in Mind of the object. When moving my eyes are directed onto the ground a little distance ahead. As I approach the object the hands get closer and closer together until over the object they are almost touching, but they never do quite touch. If I go past the object my hands tend to come apart again and then return to the start position.

While approaching the object I do not think of the hands at all, only of the object of the search in the normal way. But once the question is locked in the mind I do not have to bother with it and am able to think of other things. As I said I do not bother with the hands but I am conscious of when they are in the found position.

Direction Finding. For direction finding the hands alone can be useful too. The procedure is the same as that described for the angle rod. The arm is stretched out at the shoulder level, palm of the hand at right angles to the ground. With the object of search clearly in mind, swing round on the body axis until you 'feel' that the hand is pointing in a significant direction then swing backwards and forwards over this general direction until the exact point is found.

Note. When using the hands alone it is more than ever essential to keep the brain out of the work and allow the Mind to operate and do the work.

The Mind Alone

It is perfectly possible to use the Mind alone without any tools, but it requires much training and practice and it has many limitations in practical work. It is apt to be deceptive in practice and it is not recommended for any but experienced and qualified dowsers and these should have had much practice with it on tasks which have demonstrable results so that they know and recognise their own limitations with the method. Personally I find it unreliable.

The technique is simply to sit and answer questions thrown at one by someone else in relation to the problem to be solved. To the questions one answers quickly and without thought, Yes or No. The old expression 'He said the first thing that came into his head' has validity in this context!

An example of the use of this method is given in Part III Case 6 A lost Stone.

Counting.

I use a counting method for finding Depth, Distance, Age, Date, Quality, Quantity, Identification of minerals and for some other purposes. It is a simple method and obviates the use of any of the other methods, such as Colours, used by dowsers.

The broad application of the method is shown in this example of depthing the water in a well. This is also a useful exercise for a novice because it can be checked later by a visit to the well when the depth to the water can be measured.

The drill is as follows. Get the question clearly in mind, for example, 'What is the depth to the top of the water in this well'. If using a pendulum map dowsing, I hold it over the well where it is marked on the map and start it gyrating. When I have collected my thoughts, got the question clear and started the mind seeking the answer, I start counting down in feet visualising the top of the water in the well. The counting in feet is in time with the swing of the pendulum each rotation being one foot, or ten feet depending on the unit of measurement I am using. When my counting reaches the key depth figure the pendulum swing changes from a gyration to an oscillation. Thus what I know in my mind subconsciously, is indicated visually to me by the change in the pendulum's movement.

An interesting thing is that more often than not I feel quite clearly when I am getting close to the critical figure in the pendulum swing and this illustrates the 'knowing' of the answer in the mind. It also emphasises the importance of keeping the active brain out of these searches otherwise wishful thinking or preconceived ideas may influence the results.

When I first used this method of depthing I used to visualise a ladder going down to the top of the water and counted the rungs down. I mention this as it may help novices to get the idea of counting down in a practical way.

If I am doing on the spot dowsing with a rod I first find the object and stand over it, then proceed to count down to it as explained for the pendulum.

If working in large numbers as when depthing oil for instance I start counting in thousands of feet and have in mind, 'Is it more than 1000 ft, 2000 ft, 3000 ft, etc'. If the pendulum changes from gyration to oscillation at 7000 ft I know that the depth is between 6000 ft and 7000 ft so start counting again in hundreds from 6000 ft. If it oscillates at 6700 ft I know the depth is between 6600 ft and 6700 ft. If it is necessary to be more precise I count up from 6600 ft in 10's to get the more accurate figure.

For Dating Sites or objects I usually first establish by question and answer if it is AD or BC, but it is perfectly possible to work from the present date and get a date of 'Before Present' and this I do use for dating subjects older than about BC 5000, but I prefer the AD/BC dating for the younger periods probably because one's mind is used to that way of thinking.

If the object is AD, I count from AD in 100s and if BC, I count back from BC in 100s, in each case the query in mind is 'Is it more than AD 100, 200, 300, etc. or 'Is it more than BC 100, 200, 300,' etc. or 'Is it more than BC 1000, 2000, 3000,' etc. in each case the pendulum will continue to gyrate as I say a date, in time with the swing. When it changes to oscillation I know I am at the figure beyond the date. It is then simple to get at the more detailed date by the same method described above.

Another application is in grading the comparative value, quantity or quality of something, these I rate out of a top mark of 10. (100 can be used if you like but that involves more counting and tends to be laborious). An instance of this is in grading a sample of soil in which a crop is to be sown. If the soil is rated at 4/10 in relation to the crop I would know that additives would have to be made to that soil before it is fit to take the crop. Various uses for this rating method are mentioned in the special applications in Part II.

One other use of counting is in the identifying of minerals. From each mineral I get a different Count or Rate. If I hold the pendulum over a mineral or a precious stone and count to find the rate, it will continue to gyrate with me counting the gyrations until it oscillates and then I take the figure below that last count as the rate for that subject. If there is any doubt I work down to a decimal point. Conversely if I am seeking lodes of any mineral on a map or on the ground I can take the rate off any lodes found and if the rate is the rate for the mineral I seek well and good, but if the rate is different I can look it up in my list and probably identify it.

Most books on dowsing show the author's rating or count for various things. From my own experience and from talking to other dowsers who have worked in these fields, I think we all have our own counts for various things and our figures are different from each other.

If trying to find your own rates I suggest that to begin with you start by using samples of the actual materials or what ever it is you are working with, but later you may find that it is not necessary to have the actual material but the name of the subject written on a piece of paper will suffice.

For what it is worth the following list is a selection from my list of Rates.

Antimony	14.8	Diamond	37.3
Copper	8	Hematite	15
Gas (North Sea)	13	Lead	19.3
Iron Stone	7	Nickle	9
Manganese	11	Zinc	12.7
Tin	7.3	Potash	16
Water	4.5		
Amethyst	23		

SECTION 4.

Distant Dowsing. Ground Dowsing.

Distant Dowsing.

People are inclined to think of the dowser as working only on the ground with a rod in his hand. This is not a true picture today for most of the work of the modern dowser is done first at home by what has come to be called Distant Dowsing (my Stage 1). Later the dowser normally goes to the 'ground' and confirms by Ground Dowsing the work he has done at a distance (my Stage 2). Of course the word distant can be misleading, but it has come to mean any dowsing work not done over or in the close vicinity of what is sought.

For instance, a little while ago I mislaid a paper in my work room that I needed and although I searched the cupboard where it should have been and other places where it might have been, it obstinately hid itself from me. My wife said why not dowse for it, so I got her to try. She went to the next room and drew a plan of my work room and the furniture in it, and then by map dowsing searched for the present location of the paper. She came back in a short while, went to the cupboard and produced the paper for me. Now I call that Distant Dowsing though she was never more than 20 ft from my room. On the other hand a dowser looking for Oil, conventionally, with a rod on the ground may locate oil at 10,000 ft below him but will not call that distant dowsing! So often words are difficult but so long as we are sensible and practical and know what we mean, it doesn't matter!

Distant dowsing has come to be one of the main strengths of the modern dowser. It works at any distance round the world, at any height, at any depth, on land or sea and under the sea.

The method used is a combination of simple Question and

Answer used with Map dowsing on horizontal maps or plans or on vertical sections of them.

Virtually all dowsing is a matter of question and answer, but there has grown up a concept that Question and Answer is a method on its own when it is not, it is simply a part. It can be used on its own for some operations, but in the majority of cases it is used in distant dowsing in conjunction with maps or plans. The less that maps or plans are able to be used, the more one has to rely on the straight question and answer. The more there are maps and plans etc., the less one has to rely on just question and answer.

To the unskilled dowser and indeed to all of us, mere question and answer can be dangerous, one has so little to go on, whereas when using plans or maps as well, there is usually some picture that emerges, which from its shape and position or for other reason gives some idea of the validity or not of the work. This does allow some form of double check.

All forms of distant dowsing are tricky and one has to be careful not to be misled by brain intrusion in the form of preconceived ideas or wishful thinking. There is always need for demonstrable proof that the dowsing is true and accurate. *It is highly inadvisable to use Question and Answer alone to try to solve problems to which there is no demonstrable answer.* At best it may be just frivolous, at worst it may lead to personal delusion and if others are concerned may lead to serious trouble. For how does the operator know he is correct and not suffering from a preconceived idea, from wishful thinking, or just plain delusion, if proof of the work cannot ever be provided?

Map dowsing with question and answer enables the qualified dowser to study ground, or the seas, in any part of the world while in the comfort of his home and with all his facilities readily available. Things on or under the surface of the land or the sea and under the sea bed can be examined for such purposes as the search for Oil, Gas, Minerals, Precious Stones, Water, the location of Ships on or under the sea or on the bottom, the search for and understanding of previously unknown and existing Archaeological Sites and many other purposes, even the more mundane ones such as the search for field drains, council drains, pipes and cables and the faults in them. All these and many more.

I think I am right in saying that anything that can be done by dowsing can be done by distant dowsing and probably done in more detail and with more accuracy. The work usually should be checked by on the spot work later (this is my Stage 2) and always eventually proved by whatever method is applicable.

Much of this work depends on the existence of and accuracy of maps, plans, diagrams and charts, but these can be supplemented by improvisation when good maps of the required scale are not available. It is often simple to enlarge so as to provide a sketch map of sufficient accuracy, or to define the area by the use of longitude and latitude, or even to draw an improvised grid tied to known objects or locations. I would emphasize the point about tied to known objects and location. Everything in the world lies in relation to other things, even moving things move in relation to other things. Mostly in dowsing one is dealing with static things so if one searches areas where things are marked on plans the object of the search can be found in relation to them. Thus maps and plans can provide this search background.

There are however cases where the maps and plans either do not exist in sufficient scale or detail, or where there are no features. Examples of these are Forest, Jungle, Veldt, or the high seas. In such cases, Latitude and Longitude can be used to provide a grid on which to work. I simply draw in the required Lat. and Long. grid lines on the map or chart so that I have a grid of the sort of scale I want. Usually a 4" to 6" to the mile grid is about right, but for really detailed work it may have to be of a larger scale.

Having got the grid drawn in and the degrees and minutes written on the lines, the Mind is then focussed on that area and is able to locate itself. All things in the various rectangles of the grid are related to each other and to other things in the world. Hence when one selects a certain rectangle for search by dowsing, one is searching a known area of the earth's surface and not just an area of empty land or sea.

This same principle goes right down to the other end of the scale, when, for instance, one is searching a field for a small site, or a roadway for the line a cable with a fault in it. Everything in or under the field or the roadway will be lying in direct relationship to the boundaries of the field or the roadway so if the boundaries of the field or the edges of the pavements on the roadway are drawn accurately it should be possible to locate accurately by dowsing the object of the search. Hence one factor in map dowsing is that the accuracy of the location of the object sought will be in relation to the accuracy of the sketch or drawing used. This is one of the main reasons for the need for dowsing on the ground to check the accuracy of the distant dowsing. There is always the probability of discrepancy and it is seldom safe to work directly from the Distant dowse on drawings and plans to the proof stage. The only exception to this is when the object is very large and can be located for proof over a large area, for instance as is the case with oil.

Map dowsing and question and answer are in fact the same method as far as the mechanics of the work are concerned. In every case one is using the Mind to do the work, but sometimes it is working with a map of some sort, at other times the work comes to a series of questions and answers working to a set plan.

I give in some detail, below, an instance so that the technique can be followed and understood.

The Brooch. This is the case of a brooch that was lost in Scotland. I was living in London and was told of the details of the loss by letter. The owner had had the brooch for many years and it was of great sentimental value. I knew the owner well and was keen to help if I could, despite the fact that I seldom did this sort of work.

I had never seen the brooch but it was described as being a diamond brooch in the shape of the Argyll and Sutherland Highlanders Regimental cap badge, which I knew well. I was told that the owner had been wearing it in the morning when working in the garden for a considerable time. After lunch she had taken a son to the airport in her car, and this also I had never seen. After that she had visited a hospital and then had driven home. A little time later she noticed the brooch was missing, and she had no idea where she had lost it. At my request she had enclosed with the letter a plan of the garden, which was not small, also a plan of the house.

As a result of the Brain appreciation, as I call it, the following ideas came to mind:-

The Brooch

could be in the House.

could be in the Garden.

could have been lost at the airport.

in which case it

was in official custody there.

was in someone's possession there who had found it.

was still there unfound.

could have been lost at the hospital.

in which case it

was in official custody there.

was in someone's possession there who had found it.

was still there unfound.

had been lost out of the car somewhere on the journey.

was in possession of somebody who intended to keep it.

was in the car.

was in some place I have not thought of.

This last query I always put in as one cannot think of everything and it gives a line to work on if a negative answer is obtained from all the other queries.

These ideas were turned into short, clear questions. It is very important that the questions are clear, short and unambiguous. A wise dowser once said to me 'a woolly question gets a woolly answer.' It is not always easy to frame the question properly and care is needed.

The other factor that must be allowed for is time. In this case I wanted to know where the brooch was Now. Where it had been lost might or might not be a factor in the search, but for the moment, in order to try and eliminate some of the possibilities and so simplify the problem, I wanted if possible to find out where the brooch was Now, at the moment of my work.

In this case I did not go on speaking of the brooch as I had that as firmly in mind as possible and could visualize it. I find in all my work there comes a moment early on that the object of search gets, as it were, locked in the mind and I don't have to think about it specifically. In other cases in this sort of work where it is not easy to visualize the object clearly it sometimes is an effort to keep it clearly before me. In these, a photograph or a drawing is a help if they are accurate enough. People's verbal or written descriptions are not always easy to follow and sometimes they are liable to be inaccurate. With jewellery and with other things of which there are many of the same type, it is essential to have some form of identification which enables the dowser to differentiate the lost object from others similar or nearly so.

In cases of this sort I write the questions down spaced well apart so that they can each be considered in turn without being conscious of the others. The pendulum is then held over the question which is clearly in mind, also in mind is the Need to know the answer correctly. As I have said before, it is necessary to switch off the brain and allow the mind to feel out for the answer.

When I am ready I allow the pendulum to swing and it will swing for me as explained in section 3. Using the tools.

In this case I got a No to every question until I came to the car. The answer to this one was Yes. I had not seen the car and had no idea of its make, so I drew a diagramatic motor car thus:-

Fig 9. The rough drawing of the car used when searching for the brooch.

and proceeded to search that by map dowsing as I would any horizontal plan. I looked at the plan and allowed the mind to feel out for the brooch. The first question was 'Is the brooch in the car now?' The answer to that was Yes.

The next was 'Where is it?' In this case as the area was small I let the pendulum move slowly over the area of the car and quickly it centred over the extreme back left-hand corner. This indicated to me that the brooch was there. After various checks I decided that this was worth following up although it appeared to be an unlikely answer. I telephoned and spoke to the husband and suggested they look in the extreme left-hand back corner of the boot of the car. He said that the car was a countryman and had no boot and that the car had already been searched. He went on to say that it was now in a garage in the town for servicing. I suggested that it might be worth having a look nevertheless. A little time later I got a telegram to say that the brooch had been found exactly where I had said it was!

I have told this story in considerable detail to show some of the problems that arise. As I said at the beginning, this is not a line of work that I like but it is rewarding when it comes off. I don't find it easy and do not get a high percentage of success.

Maps, plans and drawings can be used in the search for many things. The simplest example is the one given in the above story. The drawing of the car is elementary in the extreme, but served its purpose. The search for the lost paper

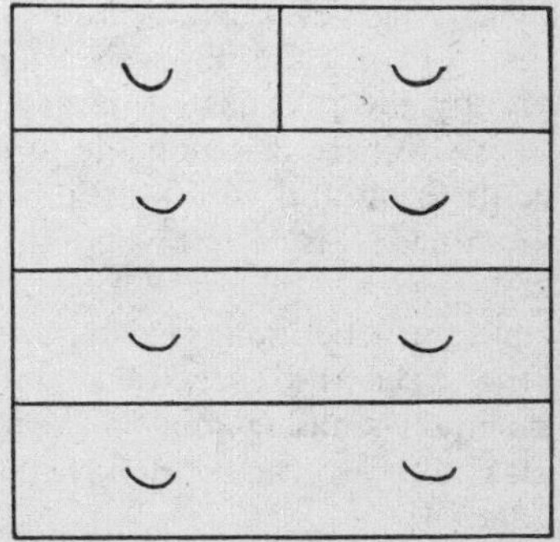

Fig 10. Sketch of chest of drawers.

mentioned earlier is also an example of the use of a simple drawing which was freehand and not to scale. In both cases a drawing is made which adequately represents the area or areas in which the object might be. The location of the object on the sketch will be accurate to the degree of accuracy of the drawing. If accuracy is not important, a sketch whether horizontal or vertical is good enough. For instance, if searching a piece of furniture which has drawers one below the other, a vertical picture can be used to determine which drawer and approximately where in that drawer in the vertical plane the object lies.

This could also be done purely by question and answer, of course, but personally I perfer to locate by a mixture of question and answer and map dowsing rather than by question and answer alone, I find it is safer.

If accuracy is necessary, the drawings must be accurate. If, for instance, a search is being made for the location of a lost object in a field of some size, it is all right to establish the fact of the object being in the field by a simple sketch, but to get an accurate location an accurate drawing of the field will have to be made before map dowsing for it.

Enlargements of portions of Maps. The initial search for something can be carried out on very small scale maps, even on a map of the world. Eventually a much larger scale of map will have to be used to get detailed location and this scale will have to be adjusted to suit the dowser's requirements. Often this can be done by the purchase of larger scale maps, but these are expensive. Where it is possible to enlarge by hand this is not difficult to do and with a little practice, adequate results can be obtained. It is easiest where the detail is mainly straight lines.

In Great Britain very good maps exist, particularly the 1" to 1 Mile, the 6" to 1 Mile and 1/2500. Enlargements from the latter two are normally simple to make. The tools required are a ruler, compass and protractor. I have also proportional dividers, an ideal tool.

For Archaeological work I use the latter two maps mostly,

and enlarge from the 6″ when possible because of the expense of the 1/2500. When enlarging from the 6″ I usually multiply by 6 and so get a scale of 36″ to 1 Mile. If in the end that is not large enough I double it or treble it. This covers most cases.

Use of Latitude and Longitude. On maps where there are few features I draw in the Latitude and Longitude lightly. I then enlarge the resulting Degree or Minute rectangles as necessary. This gives a blank series of rectangles on the paper with numbered lines. I then sketch in the necessary features of the map, for instance a road, railway, hill, river etc., putting in just enough to be able to relate the natural features to the grid. Thus any subsequent dowsing is tied in to the grid and natural features.

Use of an improvised Grid. In Great Britain there is a very good grid which is superimposed on all modern maps. It is simple to enlarge this grid and then add the salient features as described in the above paragraph.

In cases where no grid and no Latitude and Longitude is marked I draw in an improvised grid of my own, arbitrarily tied to some marked feature. The part of this grid that covers the area of interest is then enlarged as required and the salient features sketched in. (Fig 11.)

In this case the improvised grid was tied to part of the railway.

How to search a horizontal Map. The first thing to do is to find out if what is sought is in the area covered by that map. To do this, get yourself mentally in contact with the map and focussed on it. I usually look at it in general, see the area it covers, note the scale and then run my hand over it. Whether this has any direct effect I doubt, (one could call it a shibboleth) but it is part of the business of focusing the mind. If the map is large I divide it up into manageable parts. I do not mark the map to divide it up, but simply divide off an area with my hand or arm. I then hold the pendulum over each part in turn with the appropriate query in mind to see if what

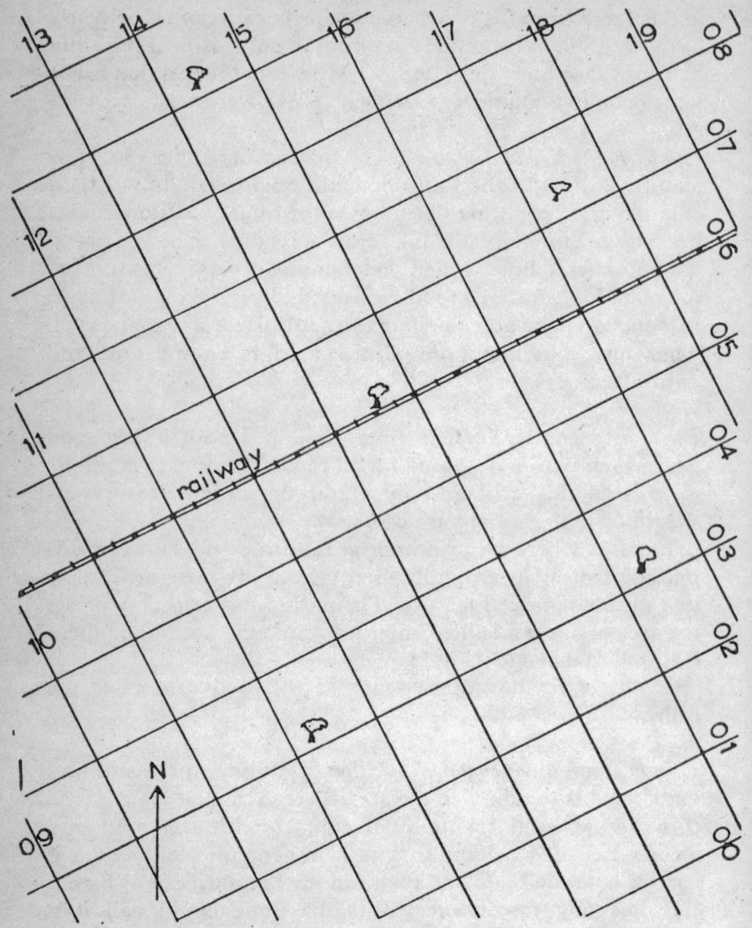

Fig 11. Improvised grid based on the railway but it could have been based on a line through two of the trees if required.

I seek is in that area. The answer should be yes or no. If the answer is yes then the next thing is to discover where it lies.

There are two ways I use for this. One is to use the detailed Area Search technique described in Section 3. This can be laborious and is best done by dividing the plan up into sections which are searched in turn, the pendulum being moved over the map, up and down or across and back in a planned way so that the whole area is covered. The other way is to use the pendulum for a Directional and Distance search which is fully described in Section 3. Details of the application of these methods to special problems such as Archaeology, minerals, drains, etc., are given in the appropriate sections later. If the scale of the map is not large enough to get the detail required then it will be necessary to enlarge the required portion of the map.

The Vertical Search. It is extremely useful to be able to do a vertical search down into the earth, down through the sea or down through the sea floor. I have made good use of this technique on many archaeological sites, in mineral search, in oil search and depthing, in geological studies and occasionally for checking the depth of water runs. As an example, once the run and width of mineral lodes in an area have been located by horizontal map dowsing, it is useful to be able to check this information by a vertical Section map dowse. This will give the depth below surface of the top and bottom of the lodes and the angle to the horizontal at which they lie, as well as a check on the thickness of the lode.

To get the information that I wanted I would draw a line P–Q at right angles through the lines of the lodes as found by the horizontal map dowse. This, say is 600 ft long. Draw a section down into the ground under P–Q using any convenient vertical scale. The vertical scale will seldom be the same as the horizontal one as it will not be convenient. No difficulty arises from this provided that it is remembered that distortion of the shape of the object will probably result. In this case all we need is the depth of top and bottom of the lodes and the angle at which the lodes are lying in the earth. The vertical scale is drawn and the depth figures are written down beside the lines to impress them on the mind.

When doing the dowsing it is essential to get clearly into the mind that one is working *vertically into* the earth and *not* horizontally, and that the lodes when located will be seen in section.

At first this may not be so easy, but after a little practice it comes quite naturally. Apart from this, the map dowsing is normal. One searches down for the top of one of the lodes and then outlines it in the normal way; then the others are outlined in a similar way.

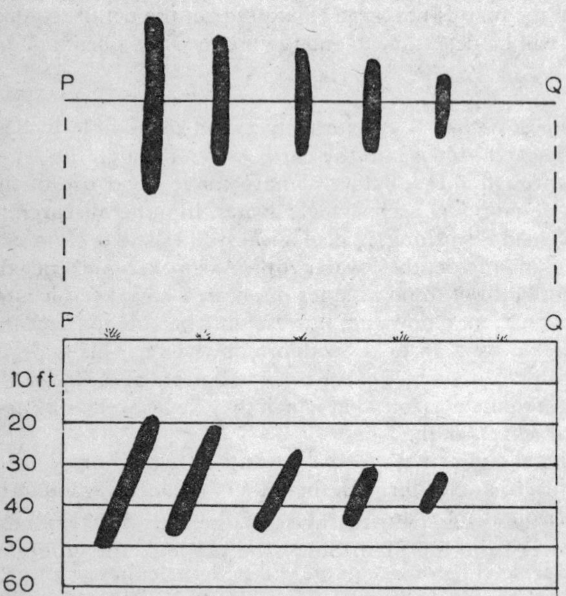

Fig 12. Horizontal plan of the top of the Lodes underground as found by dowsing together with a vertical section through the Lodes along the line P–Q. Dowsing shows the depth of the top and the bottom of the Lodes and the angle at which they lie to the vertical.

This vertical map dowse acts as a check on the findings in the original horizontal work – and vice versa. If they do not agree, search for the error.

As I said at the beginning of this paragraph, this technique has many applications and these will be mentioned in the appropriate Sections.

Ground Dowsing.

In ground dowsing one is working 'on the ground' in direct search for the object. If distant dowsing has been used the picture obtained by that can be confirmed or modified, but at the end of the ground dowse a clear picture of what is or is not there should emerge from a combination of the two. If the situation is such that proof requires later digging or drilling the exact spots where this should take place can be marked.

Any tools can be used for this stage, personally I usually use a V rod but if it happens that the area of work is too small or too cramped to enable the use of the V rod I use a pendulum, but I find this seldom happens except when working in buildings or in large ditches. Sometimes I use a Wand if searching walls or parts of buildings above waist height, or some place that is out of reach in the horizontal plane with the V rod.

Under normal circumstances distant dowsing will have been completed before coming to do the ground dowsing but even if I have never seen the ground before the general procedure would be much the same.

(a) On arrival study the map or plan of the area and compare it with the ground.

(b) Walk over the area and get the feel of it. Note any differences from the plan. Study the shape of the ground or buildings.

(c) Consider if the ground fits in with and is suitable for what is to be sought. Does the picture obtained by distant dowsing fit in with the ground or buildings and is it a feasible one?

(d) Are there any factors to be seen which may have misled me when doing the map dowse?

These are the early considerations before any dowsing is done on the ground. I then decide how to tackle the problem of confirmation of the distant dowsing.

(e) Start dowsing with a clear picture of what is sought and try to locate a definite point on the ground. It is not good enough to seek only an underground stream or a defensive ditch, for accuracy the near side of the stream or the ditch has to be located and later the far side. If you find what you seek mark the exact spot each time with a peg. I usually slope the peg in the direction in which I have been walking when the rod turned, by this means I have a check later, on the direction in which I was moving when the spot was marked. If many pegs have to be placed in a complicated area this often helps when sorting out the picture.

It is important to get into the habit of finding and marking the exact spot over what you seek, quite often a matter of a few inches may make the difference between success and failure.

(f) As you go along with the work study the picture that is emerging on the ground and consider its likeness to the distant dowsed picture. Make an occasional measurement to see if the emerging picture is roughly similar, if it is not satisfactory stop and consider. The ground work will not always be exactly the same as the distant work, as all sorts of errors can creep into the distant work. If the emerging picture seems reasonable then carry on and complete the whole.

(g) If the picture marked on the ground is satisfactory and similar to the distant dowsing and if you feel that the ground dowsing is sound, then continue to the next stage which is to take the action necessary to provide *proof* that the dowsing is correct.

(h) If the picture is unsatisfactory search for a reason. With experience you will know fairly soon if the ground dowsing feels right and in agreement with the distant work or if it does not. If something is wrong query the ground dowsing first. Are you in the correct spot on the ground that was map dowsed? Have you found what you sought despite the fact that it does not agree with the distant work? Have you made a mistake on the ground? Has there been a mistake in the distant dowsing?

It is no good going to the Proof stage, which may involve much work and perhaps expense, until you are reasonably sure that the work on the ground is sound, it is better to think again and re-do the work from the beginning.

These broad headings cover in general the ground dowsing work for many differing types of work. Further detail may be found in the sections dealing with special applications.

SECTION 5.

Samples. Colours. Remenance. Shibboleths. Mistakes.

Samples

In the older books on dowsing one reads much about Samples or witnesses as they are often called. In fact these are mind focussers only. Once the dowser is trained and knows the background of the field he is working in the sample is seldom needed. But they are useful for beginners and perhaps for trained dowsers when starting in a new field. To begin with it is not easy to get the object of search clearly in mind if one is a beginner and sometimes when one changes to something new and not easily visualised as a qualified worker, one needs some form of reminder of what one seeks, so under these conditions the sample may be needed.

On the other hand there are areas in which the sample is always essential and these are in cases where there are many of the same type as what is sought and where it is difficult to differentiate between them. Instances of these are Humans, Animals, Birds, and sometimes in Minerals. In these fields when it is necessary to distinguish between individuals a sample is often essential.

For myself when working in a known field I do not normally use samples. If I get a bit tired and have to change from considering one thing to another then I sometimes do. When working with something completely new, such as a mineral that I have not worked with before, then I may use a sample.

When using samples it is not necessary in all cases to have a sample of the actual substance, it is sufficient usually to write the name of the substance, or whatever is being sought, on a piece of paper and use this as the sample. This may sound fantastic but it works and it is no more fantastic than the fact of dowsing.

This use of the written word in place of a sample is well known, but I learnt the use of it early. When searching for archaeological sites of a certain period one did not want to be bothered with those of other periods and so a sample of the period sought should have helped. Usually one was looking for the extreme outside edge of the sites and this was normally a defensive ditch or a pallisade trench. But what is the sample for say a Roman ditch as opposed to an Iron Age one or a Medieval one? I soon found that the written sample was all that was necessary.

Where actual samples are necessary as with Humans and Animals a blood spot is the best and this lasts for life. Next best is a piece of Hair either specially cut or for instance from the combings from a hair brush. I have had no experience with pieces of finger-nail or toe-nail though it is always said that the witches of old used them effectively! Photographs of finger prints are satisfactory, they are factual representations of a personal characteristic that does not alter, but one does not often get the chance to use them. A good photograph is sometimes useful as is writing or a signature but I have had little experience with these.

If however the human or animal is well known to the dowser then a sample may not be necessary.

Colours.

Some dowsers use colours as a form of sample or a form of identification. For this they usually use the Mager rosette which has eight colours marked on it, Violet, Blue, Green, Yellow, Red, Grey, Black, White.

They associate things sought with differing colours. For instance when the quality of a sample of water has to be tested the dowser will associate the varying qualities of water with different colours for instance:-

Good drinking	White
Unfit for drinking	Black
Suitable only for washing	Grey

Each dowser makes up his own coding and I have met all sorts of variants even of the above.

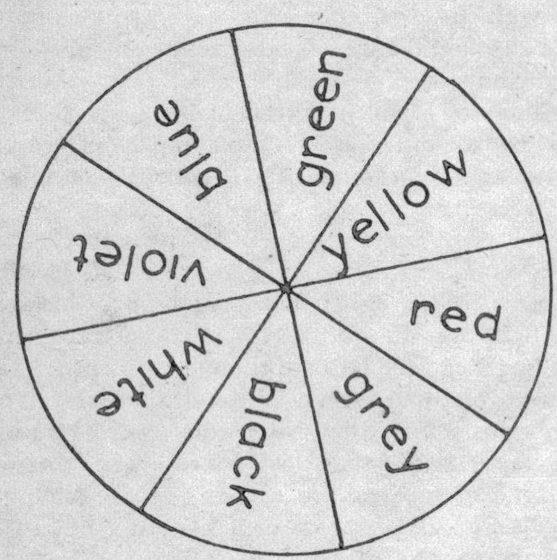

Fig 13. The Mager Rosette.

I mention colours only because they are used by many dowsers and may be of use to beginners. Personally I never use them and get my results by other means.

Remenance.

This is a phenomenon which is encountered in dowsing and it is one of the things that is not understood. It would seem that if a living or an inanimate object has been in a certain place and moves or is moved away, it seems to leave behind something of itself that can be picked up by the dowser. It is as if it left behind a 'scent'. It is a matter of interest that the Hunas apparently used to visualise every living thing as leaving a very fine thread behind as it moved on.

By dowsing, the route taken by a person or thing can be followed and its present whereabouts ascertained. In searching for things that can move or may have been moved it is essential to include the time factor. If this is not done mistakes in location can easily be made. 'Where is X *now*' or 'Where was X at 0900 hours' are the sort of questions that should be framed. Another instance is in the search for oil. In many places oil formed and lay in the ground but later due to earth movement it either drained away or was burnt up and changed in composition. In these places the dowser may be misled into thinking that oil is still there unless he questions whether it is there now.

Shibboletns.

We come now to what I call shibboleths, defined as 'Old fashioned and generally abandoned doctrine once held essential.' I have to be careful here because I have no wish to tread on toes or to change people's beliefs. My only wish is to simplify dowsing for the beginner.

The books and writings about dowsing are full of shibboleths and one comes across all sorts of pet ideas which have been adopted and have become a firm part of technique and once part of the technique they are not easily uprooted. Nor indeed is there need for the dowser to change his beliefs if the technique works for him, even though it makes his working more complicated.

On the other hand it must be realised that if a dowser thinks that doing a thing a certain way may prevent him finding what he seeks by dowsing the thought is sufficient to inhibit him and he will not be able to find what he seeks because of this self imposed belief which acts as a form of mental block. Conversely if he firmly believes he can find what he seeks despite all sorts of difficulties it is more than likely that he will do so.

Dowsing is difficult enough without cluttering it up with beliefs which have no validity and I am sure we should make it as simple as is possible, hence the need to look at these ideas and be rid of them.

Many of them stem from the older concept of dowsing as a purely physical operation picking up emanations from the ground and elsewhere. We now know there is more to it than that.

When a learner, I was brought up with all these ideas but for one reason or another I have abandoned them long since. Here are a few of them:-

'Don't wear rubber boots or composition soles when dowsing'. This stems from the concept of the dowsing force rising from the ground through the feet being unable to pass through the insulation of the rubber sole. Working as a dowser over the hills in Scotland and elsewhere I have perforce used rubber boots for many many hours and have never noticed any difference.

'Keep both feet on the floor'. I do not know where this originated, but it is probably based on the concept of the rising force again. It is sufficient to note that when walking and doing a dowsing job, more time is spent with one foot off the ground than with two on it! Also Dowsing works perfectly well from a car and from an aeroplane.

'When Map dowsing always face West (or North, South or East)'. I think this stems from the idea that it is important to keep in some particular relationship with the earth forces. Long ago the room I had to work in and the furniture that I had, did not permit me to do what was advised and I found that it made no difference at all.

'Always orientate the map before dowsing'. This also stems from this earth force effect. I very soon found that the bit of the map that I wanted to work on was often the part furthest away from me, so I turned it round (I must admit with trepidation the first time!) and the Dowsing worked just as well!

Nowadays when working out the details of an

archaeological site by map dowsing, the setting of the map or plan is changed repeatedly as I move it round as I wish, to get at the detail of the various parts.

'Don't Dowse before 10 am or after sundown'. This belief must be something to do with earth forces and the sun. It is sufficient to say that one dowser that I know states that he always does his best work after dark. For myself I do not find that it makes much difference, the state of my freshness or tiredness is the governing factor.

'Don't pierce the paper on which you are map dowsing'. This I suppose is another earth force idea. I can assure you that a hole in the paper has no effect on my work. But if I believed it did, it might.

I have already mentioned in Section 3 two other possible shibboleths, one the idea that the longer the rod the more sensitive and the other that one might get a taste in the mouth when dowsing over water.

With these few instances I hope to make the point. We all probably have our own shibboleths but my advice to novices is to question then avoid such beliefs and keep the dowsing simple. Once you accept a shibboleth you are apt to be stuck with it, so beware. (I wonder if you walk under ladders or turn your money to the new moon?!)

Mistakes.

Mistakes in dowsing arise from a variety of reasons and it is important that the dowser tries to find the reasons for failure for by so doing he will get to know the likely causes of his failures and be able to guard against them in the future.

I give below some of the more common causes of failure.

Preconceived Ideas. Wishful Thinking. I put these top of the list as I believe these are a cause of failure to many people at any stage of their career but particularly in their early training days. It is essential to be completely neutral when operating the pendulum, the rod or any of the tools. The question is framed and the search starts but the dowser must be in the sort of frame of mind while he is dowsing that does not mind if the object he seeks is there or not, he must be completely neutral. If he allows his own wishes and ideas to come into the business of finding he is using his brain and not his Mind alone, as he should.

Carelessness and Haste. I put these next as a cause of failure. It never pays to hurry over the preparation of a job nor over the execution of it. Time spent over the preparation for a job and the appreciation of the problem is never wasted. This applies equally to distant dowsing as well as to on the spot dowsing. For all successful work the mind has to be fully informed and relaxed and the body reasonably so. For instance it is usually a mistake to drive a car a long way then start dowsing immediately, I find I need time to settle back and relax.

Lack of contact' with the ground in the area of work. I find it helps to spend a little time walking over the ground in the area of the job particularly if the country is new to me, it allows me to get the 'feel' of that portion of the country. Sub-soils vary enormously and I think it is a good thing to get the feel of what is the sub-soil in the area of work. This applies to distant dowsing on maps, as well as to work on the spot. Neglect of this acclimatisation can lead to errors.

Effect of certain soils. It is always said that water finders have difficulty in depthing through clay. Whether this is a shibboleth or a truth I do not know but clay can be difficult for me to work over in even comparatively shallow archaeological work. Deepish sand can also be difficult. With either sand or clay I have to be careful. For some reason that I do not understand, when map dowsing over these I am liable to get a pattern due to, or something to do with, the clay and the sand themselves and nothing to do with the anomalies being sought. There is a similar difficulty when dowsing on the ground in such areas and the same misleading pattern of reactions seem to come up. There may be some quite simple explanation to this perhaps to do with water or moisture in the clay and sand: However knowing of this possible reaction I can avoid it.

Mistaking Natural things for what is Sought. Soil and Strata changes, Faults, Banks of Gravel and patches of it, these can all cause mistakes of identification. These often give linear patterns and can be mistaken for other things if the dowser is careless or inexperienced in that sort of work. The defence against this is to be clear about what you are looking for and allow nothing else to intrude, also in addition it is as well to have some other means of identifying what you have found.

Lack of Identification. It is not difficult to mistake one thing for another and not only natural things. For instance a deepish field drain can be mistaken for the remains of a defensive ditch. In my work in the early days water lines used to intrude and I seemed to pick them up by mistake when looking for other things, but this seldom happens now as I know the feel of water with my tools, it is different from other things. It is important for the dowser to develop alternative dowsing means so that he can check by other means what he has found.

The Time Factor. If time is a factor in the work it is essential to recognise this and allow for it. If for instance you are searching for a missing article it is probably necessary to know where the object of search is Now. Where the loss occurred, where the object was yesterday and where it is now may be three different places, so unless the Now is included in the question it is possible to pick up yesterday's position and think it is today's. (see Remenance).

Insufficient Background Knowledge and Experience. This last but not least factor is a cause of many failures. The dowser must know the background of the subject he is working in. Until he does he will be liable to make stupid and unnecessary mistakes.

A & N Other. I suggest you jot down the cause of your own mistakes in the space below this if they are different from the above, just to remind you! !

PART II

SECTION 6.

Archaeology.

This is my own special application of dowsing and as few others have so far made use of it for practical archaeological work this section will contain considerable detail and experience.

It is not difficult to find, by dowsing, completely unknown sites where nothing shows on the surface of the ground and where there is no tradition of anything in the vicinity, to outline them in considerable detail and to date them.

There is no doubt whatever that if professional archaeologists used dowsing means to find and then to outline their sites and date them, they would save enormously in time and money and would also quicken the process of finding out about where and how people have lived in the past.

For the dowser it is necessary to learn a certain outline of archaeology, but much of this can be acquired over the process of time. However, the sooner the essentials are learnt the better. It is quite hopeless looking for archaeological sites when you have no idea what you are looking for and faulty elementary knowledge will often lead to mistakes in practice and in deduction.

It is necessary to know the general outline of the periods, the type and shape of the buildings and monuments of those periods and in addition what is likely to be left of them in the ground today. Something of how people lived and what they were able to do is also important.

It is essential to be able to disentangle by shape, date and possible use what remains in the ground of sites of all sorts, buildings and other man-made things in general. These can often be simple in layout but sometimes become very complex when the periods that remain overlap on the same site.

The use of dowsing in archaeology is not just a matter of finding bits of pottery, or the odd valuable artifact! Its proper use is in finding sites, dating them so that the period is known and then working out sufficient of the outline of the site in general to assist in its later excavation which in the end provides the only acceptable *proof* of what is there and its date.

Having said all this the dowser should not be put off starting in this field. When I started I had practically no knowledge, but I did have good friends who helped me to learn in theory and in practice on the ground. It is best to start small and satisfy yourself that you can find man-made anomalies in the ground without getting mixed up with natural anomalies. From the beginning it is essential to be prepared to get proof of your dowsing, usually this can only be obtained by the use of the spade.

If you intend to do your own excavations, however small, you must be able to do them properly and be able to recognise what you find, so go and learn by attending and working in excavations run by qualified people. Also learn how to record what you find by drawings, photographs and the written report. The local archaeological society should be a help, so be in touch with them.

Before going over ground it is essential to see the farmer and often the landowner for permission to go over the ground. If approached tactfully and in consideration of crops there is seldom any difficulty. In my experience most farmers are greatly interested in anything which lies under their ground.

The Distant Dowsing work. The first need is a map, plan or drawing. To make it simpler I shall always refer to maps but this will imply drawings and plans or whatever is used.

Large scale maps are very expensive nowadays, they used to be inexpensive enough to allow map dowsing directly on to the face of the map but today they are too valuable for that use. It is best to use copies of the map, either copies made by hand drawing or an enlargement of a small area, or a photo copy of part or all of the map sheet. Another way is to use a thin sheet of paper, thin enough to see through, which is placed over the map and secured with clips, the map dowsing markings can then be made on the paper as if on the face of the map whose features will show through the paper. Tracing paper can be used but for some reason I do not like it for this, shibboleth perhaps?!

If desirable, salient and relevant features like roads, fences and grid lines can be traced through on to the paper. Always put a name to the area on the paper, a map reference, a scale, the north point and setting marks so that the paper can be re-positioned exactly on the map as it was when the map dowse was being done. More than once I have come across, among my papers, interesting markings on a piece of paper which has obviously been used for a map dowse but on which there is no reference to show where it belongs and now I find I simply cannot remember where it belongs!

The maps of Great Britain are good. I find the 1" to 1 Mile is very good for getting a general picture by dowsing of such things that are large in area or have some length like old roads. The 6" on the other hand is usually the best map to start with if the general area of search is known, the detail is good and much of it can be enlarged manually if required, but of course most sites will be too small to get much of a picture of them at the 6" scale. A medium sized Roman Fort at that scale can be recognised as a rectangle but not much detail can be obtained.

When enlarging the 6" I usually enlarge to 36" to 1 Mile, this gives a good size of scale which allows most sites to be map dowsed in some detail. If I require a larger picture to work on later I double or treble the above scale and re-dowse the site. If the location of the site is known the ideal map to start on is the 1/2500, on this quite small sites will come up in sufficient size to be marked in detail and if greater detail is required further enlargement can be made. (For further details of maps and enlargements see Section 4. Distant dowsing).

The Search by Map Dowsing. Usually one seems to be looking either for sites of a certain period, or searching to see if there is any site of any kind in a limited area.

If searching for sites of a certain period one has to be very selective and be clear in mind as to the type or date, for there are innumerable unknown sites of all ages and types under the soil of Great Britain and other countries. Sometimes the shape and kind of site will be unknown and one then has to be very careful and work only with a clear date period and an open mind. Usually the period will be known so the first essential is to be able to date a site as soon as indications of one are found, for it is a pity to have to waste time on sites that are not required. (For dating procedure see Section 3. Counting).

If on the other hand one is searching a limited area for any site of interest as a novice might, or if a new road was to cross an area, or if a farmer wanted to know if there was anything of interest under his land, then the search is for any archaeological site. In these circumstances do not be content with the first you find, there may be others. Should a complex site be found the date obtained from it will probably be the date of the latest site occupation, in such a case it is worth trying to establish the shape of the other periods and their date.

When searching for sites I always look for the outside edge and establish that first, then get the date to see if it is a suitable date for the purpose. I then work out the outside edge in detail complete with the breaks in it. These breaks may be entrances with tracks running away from them and these I often find help to identify the type of site, they are also often a help in marking out the limits of the site. For instance in Fig 14(a) I have picked up the outside edge of the main domestic area but have missed the fence outside it of which today only the post holes remain. The clue to the probability of some other feature was the straightness and depth of the entrance coupled with the change in direction of the track outside the fence. This sort of road entrance picture coupled with the depth, is often a guide to the area covered by the defences of the site

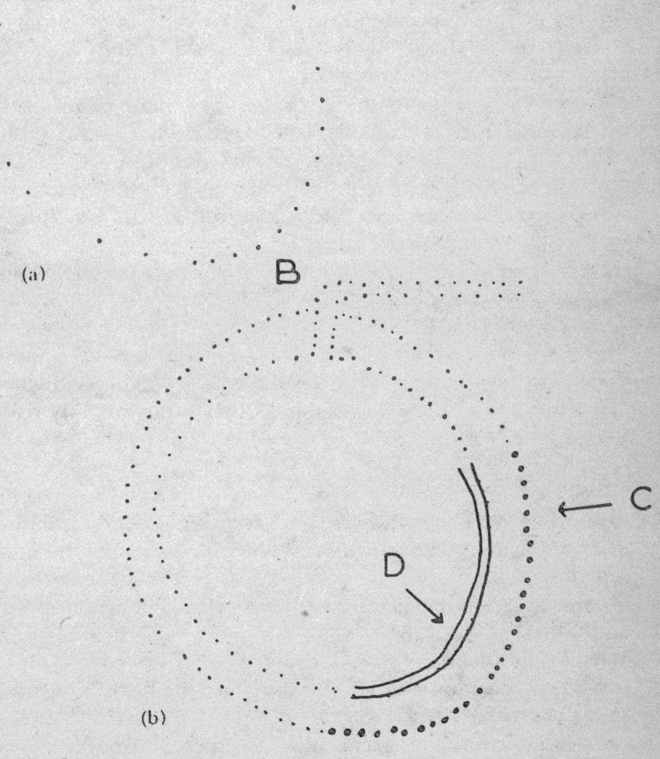

Fig 14. The drawings (a) and (b) represent parts of a composite site drawn to illustrate the text.
A. represents an outside edge as first found by dowsing.
B. Shows the outer fence marked in.
C. Shows Post Holes.
D. Shows the edges of the pallisade Trench.

After getting the outside edge marked clearly I then see if it has any width. If it appears to have no width I know that it is probably just a simple fence of some sort, where only the post holes remain. I then test to find the post holes in the line of this fence (Fig 14 (C)). These are not difficult to find by working carefully round the line of the fence thinking of the post holes. With me the pendulum tends to try to centre on them and will not flow past them freely as it would along a clean uninterrupted line. If the scale is large enough and the holes are large I can outline them individually or if more convenient, an occasional one. My added check to see if what I have found is really a post hole, is that with me the pendulum will gyrate in the opposite direction from normal over such things as post holes, stone holes, cavities and underground tunnels, this is part of my own code language.

If the outside edge has width, then it could be one of the following:-

A Pallisade Trench. (Fig 14 (D)). This when dowsed will always show width and depth but the post holes in it will probably not show when looked for by dowsing as they will probably have fallen in.

A Defensive Ditch. This will show clearly with its width and its depth. The fact of a defensive ditch or ditches can be confirmed by doing a vertical section across the run of them.

Masonry. The remains of the footing of a wall or a building will usually be straight but there are a number of occasions when the wall may be on a curve. The fact of masonry can be cross checked by question and answer, by depthing or by a vertical section across the site.

When depthing on archaeological sites I usually count down in inches but if the depth is likely to be over three feet I start counting in feet and then get the final figure in feet and inches.

Having got the shape, width and depth of the outside edge I usually try to confirm the date again. Sometimes there is good indication of approximate age by the shape and characteristics of the layout and construction, but this is not always reliable as there are many nearly similar types of construction down the ages, so I date by dowsing means and if this does seem to tie in with the type and shape I am fairly happy about it, but proof can only come by excavation. I do find that the accuracy of this rather startling method of dating is surprisingly high, it does seem to be not too difficult to get the period correct and a reasonable date within that period.

When I have got the shape of the site and an approximate date by map dowsing I then know what I think I have found and can choose whether to investigate the detail. If further detail is needed it will often involve enlarging the drawing of the area round the site and re-dowsing the whole thing again. This may sound laborious but it is often exciting to see how detail of the interior of the site and further detail of the exterior come up and what a good picture can be obtained. This final picture can be of enormous value when planning trial cuts to prove the site and also in the planning for a full excavation. (See Case 11. Chievely and Case 13. Daviot).

So by the end of the map dowse the outline of the site and much of its characteristics could be available in plan in relation to the surrounding natural features. In addition the approximate depth below present surface should be known as well as the size and shape of defensive ditches, pallisade trenches etc., and the entrances and possibly the tracks leading to them if they still exist. These tracks can be useful as they often lead to other similar sites.

The Ground Dowse. Next comes the ground dowse, to provide confirmation of what has been found by distant dowsing and to enable a place to be found where eventually a trial cut can be made so as to prove the existence of the site.

Here again I work to get the outside edge of the site marked first, both the line of it and its width, what it consists of and the date The general method is given in Sections 3 and 4. If this agrees in general with the distant dowsed picture I go on to get any further information I can get by ground dowsing, such as the entrances and the tracks running from the site which may be useful. I usually check these features for date also, to make sure that all are of the same period.

It is not possible to get nearly as much detail by ground dowsing as it is by distant dowsing, so it does not pay to try to get it and indeed it may lead to confusion. At this stage provided the distant dowsing has been satisfactory the ground dowsing is only to try to get confirmation in general that a site of the required period is there and such detail as one tries to get is only to get further confirmation before embarking on a trial cut.

If a site is a complex one with more than one period mixed up with another it is best to confirm by finding one simple feature or one period, such as a defensive ditch and prove that. More than ever is it a mistake to try to work out this sort of site by ground dowsing alone, or at this stage to try to unravel the intricacies of the inside by ground dowsing. Once a feature has been proved and identified it is then fairly simple to follow it by dowsing and prove it further on, by this means the complex site can be unravelled.

Sometimes one has to do the ground dowsing without having done any distant dowsing. On these occasions one can only hope to get a simple feature outlined, perhaps part of the extreme outside edge, it is a mistake to attempt to get much detail. Unless I am forced to do without the distant dowsing I always do that first before attempting work on the ground.

The Trial Excavation. Trial cuts must be carefully placed. The object of the cut is to demonstrate that a site of the period exists there. To this end the cut must show recognisable features and if possible dateable ones, although this is not always possible. The cut must not be placed where valuable evidence may be destroyed due to lack of knowledge of the type of site and how to excavate it. It is for this reason that I always try to place the first trial cut over the outside edge of the site if it appears to be a recognisable feature and never anywhere on the inside. Usually the outside edge is a recognisable archaeological feature, a defensive ditch, a pallisade trench, a wall footing, or a series of post holes and with these one can do no great harm through lack of knowledge of the particular site.

These cuts are always done by me and are small and usually of the order of 4 ft by 10 ft initially and extended if necessary. I do not like others doing my trial cuts as if they should turn out to be unproductive one never knows whether it was the dowsing, the placing of the cut, or the execution of the excavation work that was faulty!

Incidentally I know of no greater thrill than finding what I expected from the dowsing, beginning to appear in the trial cut just under where my dowsing pegs marked the expected position. It is a real satisfaction.

See also for Archaeological Dowsing.

Part 3. Case 4. Swinbrook.
7. Walkerdales.
8. Gledenholm.
9. Rookwood.

SECTION 7.

Water.

All professional and other successful water finders have their own way of working and for the novice it may help to get in touch with one. But those who have to start on their own may find these notes helpful.

Those who wish to become water finders (I do not like the term water Diviners) must know a certain amount about Geology and understand how water lies in and travels in the ground. How it lies in the ground depends on the various types of strata, and the angle at which they lie and the breaks and changes in and between the various strata. Broadly speaking water may lie in gravelly areas and in large pools in limestone and certain other strata, but in most other places it lies and moves in comparatively narrow streams. Sometimes these streams can be very narrow indeed and there an error of one foot in the dowsing might make the difference between success and failure when drilling takes place.

The dowser is usually looking for running water in streams and the problem from his point of view is to locate the stream accurately, its width, depth below surface, direction of flow, quantity flowing past a point per hour, and the quality of it in relation to the use to which the water is to be put. He must also be able to forecast the availability of that flow throughout the year, that is to say 'will the required quantity always be available?'

The dowser must also be conversant with the local government laws and rules about use of water supplies.

The first thing he has to establish is the quantity and quality of water required by the client, and the area in which it is wanted, also whether it is to be a well supply or piped.

The next stage is to discover if there are underground water streams to be tapped which will supply that quantity and quality all the year round, at a reasonable distance from the point at which it is required.

The dowser must also be able to estimate for the client the cost of drilling and be able to suggest the type of extraction system and its probable running costs. To this extent therefore he will have to have sufficient practical engineering knowledge relating to this particular field.

Once the area of search for the water is known it is advisable to study the geological map of the area and get to know generally the types of strata likely to be found there. In some countries geological maps are good and will be helpful, in other areas they may be very small scale, possibly inaccurate, or even non existent. Even in areas where much detail is given they cannot be more than a help.

The next stage is to get maps of sufficiently large scale covering the possible area of search. The 6" is quite a good scale to use, but if a larger scale is needed either a hand enlarged part of the 6" can be used or a 1/2500 purchased.

The map dowsing for the line of any stream is straightforward. The points to have in mind and on which the dowsing questions are eventually based are these:-

(a) Surface water is usually not required or wanted as it is apt to be polluted. I include streams down to 10 ft as surface water, but this will depend on local conditions.

(b) If the quality of the water matters then only good quality water is required. If the quality does not matter, for instance if it is required only for some industrial purpose, then streams not suitable for drinking purposes can be found and used.

(c) If the quantity required is comparatively small such as for domestic purposes in a house, streams that are not large can be used as long as they are of the required quality. But if required for a farm with large herds, larger quantities will be required so the smaller streams will usually be of no use. For industrial purposes very large quantities will be required so large streams will have to be found and used.

(d) It is not possible normally to extract more than a certain proportion from any underground stream, so the flow of the stream must be much greater than the quantity required to be extracted.

The problem is then studied by the dowser and the appropriate questions framed. Such a question in the early stages might be 'Where is the nearest stream of good water, running at over 1000 gallons per hour, at not less than 15 ft below surface'. Then use one of the methods of search with the pendulum on the map. Having found a point on the line of a stream get two more points and so establish part of its line of flow, then test for depth, width, direction of flow, and quality.

Depth is found by counting down as described in Section 3.

The volume of flow is found by the same method. I usually start by establishing if it is over 1000 gph, this eliminates the small streams if they are not required, and go on counting until the volume of flow is established. If smaller streams are being used I would count in 100's or 10's.

Direction of flow is found by me as follows:-

(a) With hands alone. Walking up stream with hands in the Start position the hands come together into the Found Position. Walking down stream with hands in the Start Position they remain in this position.

(b) With the pendulum both on the map and on the ground, if it is moved up stream it gyrates. If moved down stream it will oscillate in the direction of the flow.

(c) With the V rod, if moved up stream in the Start Position it will drop to the Found Position after a pace or two. If moved down stream in the Search position it stays in that position.

(d) With the angle rods, if moved up stream held in the Search Position they will, after a pace or two, come to the Found Position. If moved down stream in the Search Position they will stay in that position.

Section 3 describes my tool movements. For other people the tool movements may be quite different but it is up to the dowser to find his own code language movements for his tools so that he can differentiate between moving them up stream and down stream.

To find the quality of the water I use a rating system (Section 3, Counting) which gives marks out of 10, which figure denotes high class drinking water. Anything above 5 is drinkable while 5 and below is water to be avoided for drinking purposes. Any refinements such as Salinity can be found out by a combination of question and answer and a rating. As I said in Section 3 this system of rating I use for many purposes where comparative values etc. have to be obtained.

Some dowsers use a colour system for classifying the quality of water. They each select their own colour to represent various qualities of water such as:-

Black	Undrinkable (I have met dowsers who use black for high class water and white for bad)
White	Good for human drinking
Grey	Not very good
Blue	Saline
	etc. etc.

Each dowser has to work out his own system for himself. I like mine for my own work, I find it is applicable to many problems and is very flexible.

Having established depth, width, direction of flow, quantity of flow and quality of stream, and found these suitable, the line of the flow is plotted in detail. If the line of flow provides a suitable spot for a well or for drilling, then it looks as if this stream may provide the solution to the problem. But while working over the map it is prudent to search for other streams if they exist, so that there is something to fall back on if the original one is found later to be unsuitable for any reason.

But if the streams found are, individually, not sufficient to meet the need it may be possible to find two streams that cross over each other at differing depths so that a bore can tap both.

Equally a spot below the junction of two streams may be a useful place to find as the volume below the junction will be higher than either of the individual streams, so in the initial search record streams at different levels and stream junctions and the changes of volume of flow.

Having done all this work by distant dowsing the dowser can then go to the ground with a very good picture of what there is under the ground and he will know pretty well where to look for his water.

On the ground he will first search for the line of the stream and then check the width, depth, volume of flow and quality and compare these results with those given by the distant dowsing. If they correspond he can go ahead and taking into account the client's needs, can mark the exact spot to be drilled.

The marking of the exact spot to be drilled is important. The spot should be selected with great care and arrangements made for the driller to use that exact spot and not another. Failures sometimes occur due to the dowser's marked drill point not being used. As I said earlier there are places where an error of one foot may cause a failure.

In cases where no map dowse has been done the same procedure will be followed as was used for the map dowse. The streams will have to be found by direction and distance finding methods outlined in Section 3 and then tested for width, depth, volume and quality. This is a slow and sometimes laborious business if the area is difficult geographically or if suitable streams are hard to find. There is no doubt that distant dowsing can save a great deal of time and effort and does simplify the solution of difficult problems.

Oddments. There are one or two matters about water finding which should be mentioned.

(a) Identification. It is essential to be able to identify what one has found by rod or other tool action, whether on the map or on the ground. For me the count I get over water is 4½ so at any time I can make sure that what I am reacting to is in fact water and not something else. It is also possible to check what one has found by Question and Answer as well, so this gives a second method of check. When working on a map I can now usually recognise when I have picked up the line of a water stream by the reaction of the pendulum. I can only say that the feel of the pendulum reaction to water is different from the feel over another object, for instance oil, or the edge of an archaeological site. Over water the feel is light and active while over oil the reaction is slower and heavier. This is purely a personal reaction and is only mentioned as a matter of interest.

(b) Water finders very often talk about 'bands' of reaction that they can pick up with their tools on either side of the line of an underground water stream. These bands are said to lie parallel to the line of the stream and at varying distances from it. Some say they can calculate the depth below surface of the stream from the distance of one of the bands from the centre of the stream and from the location of another band the volume of the flow. The number of bands on either side of a stream seems to vary with each stream and each dowser, sometimes they seem to find a considerable number. It is also said that these bands can be mistaken for the actual stream itself unless care is used. This is one of the reasons why it is important to find the width of a stream as if it has width what has been found cannot be a band as they have no width.

I have always carefully avoided recognition of any form of band in my dowsing and look on them as a dangerous nuisance. If looking for water I deal directly with the edges of the stream itself only and avoid anything to do with bands. When working in other fields of dowsing, Oil, Minerals, Archaeology etc., I have never come across any form of 'bands'

(c) One usually thinks of water running in streams under the ground but there are occasions when it moves vertically upwards, either in what are called springs coming up under pressure from reservoirs under ground or from very deep sources where steam is forced up through fissures and as it rises is converted to water at the cooler levels and finally either emerges on the surface as water and runs away downhill, or it reaches a level of strata where it acts as if on the surface. On these latter occasions the water may run underground in more than one direction. When dowsing such places on a map or on the ground the area where the water stops flowing upwards will be found to be near circular. I mention this as it is sometimes disconcerting to novices to find that the source of a stream appears to be underground and circular.

SECTION 8.

Oil

The search for Oil by normal scientific means is usually extremely expensive, has to cover wide areas and is time consuming. Even when suitable strata is discovered there is no scientific means by which the geologist can say if the oil is still there in fact, before drilling takes place.

The search for oil by a dowser qualified in that field can be carried out by distant dowsing in a matter of hours. This search should be able to cover a very wide field and, at the end, produce a small area only to be searched for confirmation by the normal scientific means. Ground dowsing is not normally necessary as the area covered by the oil is comparatively large, and small errors of location do not effect the issue.

The dowser should also be able to give the depth of the oil whether on land or under the sea, a relative estimate of the quantity and quality and also an idea of the porosity of the strata in which the oil lies. Most important of all he should and must be able to confirm that the oil is in fact still there now.

To do this he must know something of the geology of oil and he needs practice and experience in dowsing in this field. The ideal team in oil search is the geologist and dowser working together.

My own work in this field has largely been experimental, but I have had the benefit of working with a geologist.

Early in 1973, before most of the oil fields of the North Sea had been found, I produced an oil map of part of the area at a scale of 1" to 15 miles. In that first search I looked only for the outside edge of areas that might contain oil, and made no effort to work at the larger scales or to locate the oil in detail. The areas outlined were those I thought worthy of search in detail. In most cases these areas were about 15 miles in diameter though some were larger. Since then, the various oil finds have been recorded on an overlay of this map and the results are very interesting and in many ways satisfactory.

In addition to the location of the oil areas, I rated them quantifically in relation to Ekofisk, which by then was well publicised. The rating was out of 10 as described in Section 3, Counting. Ekofisk I rated as 5/10, and the scale of values in relation to quantity/quality on a commercial basis were as follows:–

9/10	Excellent
8/10	Excellent
7/10	Very Good
6/10	Good
5/10	Average Good.
4/10	Not good. In the North Sea not good enough as there are better places. In areas where extraction is much easier and where oil is badly needed, it might be worthwhile working.
3/10	Not worth drilling.

Fig 15 shows part of my oil map. The chain ringed areas are those that, early in 1973, I thought were worth examining in detail. The figure in each ringed area is my forecast rating, out of 10, of the worth of the oil in that area.

I have superimposed on the map the subsequently discovered fields and oil strikes with their names. These are marked in black. The unnamed oil strikes are shown as a small black circle.

The authority of these locations is the 1976 edition of 'The Oilman Off Shore Map'.

Below are given a list of the fields and oil strikes which have been found in my marked areas shown in this portion of my map.

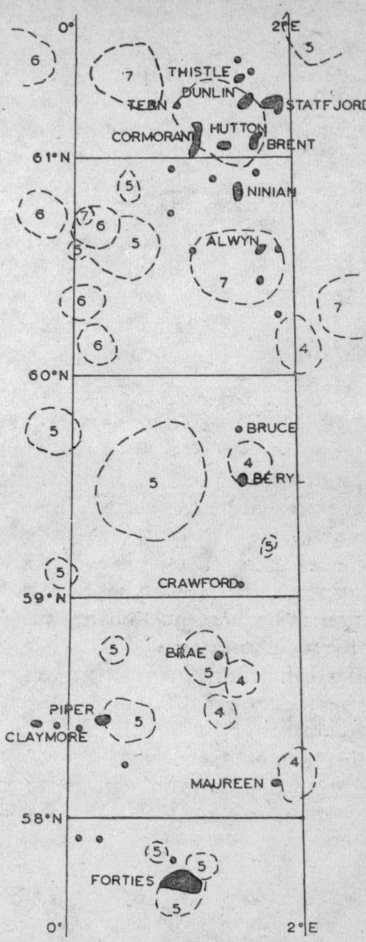

Fig 15. This is a trace of part of my original 1973 Oil map of the North Sea. The rings show areas considered worth detailed search for oil. The figures in the rings give the rating out of 10. Superimposed are the dotted areas marking the later publicised locations of the known fields with their names. The small dotted areas with crosses mark the location of other later publicised oil strikes.

Rating.	*Field.*
7/10	Hutton.
	Dunlin.
	Cormorant
	Tern.
	Brent.
7/10	Alwyn.
	3 unnamed strikes.
4/10	Beryl.
5/10	Brae.
5/10	Piper.
5/10	Forties.
4/10	Maureen.

Since 1973 I have done intermittent work on oil search both on land and under the sea and this has led me to produce a different technique which gives much more detail and reduces considerably the area to be searched by the normal scientific means. Fig 16 (a), (b), (c) show this in some detail.

The area selected is south of the Isles of Scilly and as far as I know no serious work in oil search has been done there yet, so there is no proof of its existence, however the drawings will serve to show the technique.

The first search was made on map Fig 16 (a). The result of this work seemed to show that oil does exist there now in commercial quantities at a depth of about 5000 ft. The markings on this map are mere dots.

The second study was done on map Fig 16 (b) which is at a scale four times larger than Fig 16 (a). At this scale it is possible to differentiate between oil areas as regards location, indications of size and comparative quantities of oil in each area. Some areas appear to be worth only 4/10 whereas others rate at 6/10.

The third stage was to enlarge the drawing of the area again to about four times that of Fig 16 (b) and again map dowse for the oil. At this size Fig 16 (c) a reasonable picture of each oil area can be obtained and the value of the differing parts of each can be assessed. Some idea can also be obtained of the best areas within the field to work on

Plate II. Angle Rods in Search Position. Some dowsers use only one Rod. (Copyright J.A. Muskett)

Plate III. Working with a pendulum over a Map.

Plate IV. Angle Rods in Found Position. (Copyright J. A. Muskett)

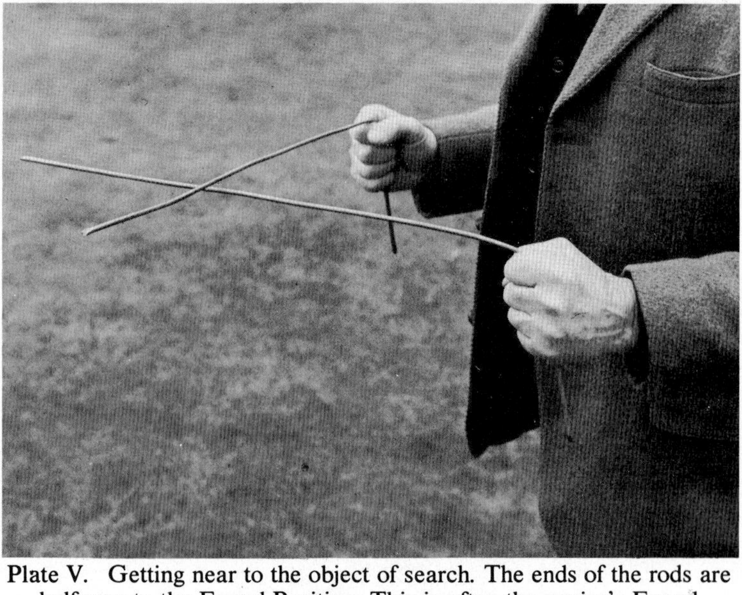

Plate V. Getting near to the object of search. The ends of the rods are half way to the Found Position. This is often the novice's Found Position. (Copyright J. A. Muskett)

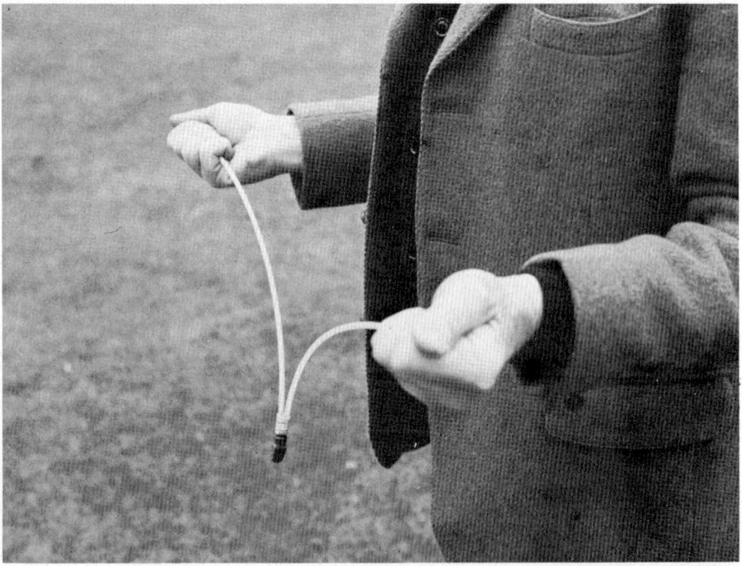

Plate VI. The V Rod in the Found Position. For the Search position see Plate I, Frontispiece. (Copyright J. A. Muskett)

Plate VII. The Start Position using the hands alone. (Copyright J. A. Muskett)

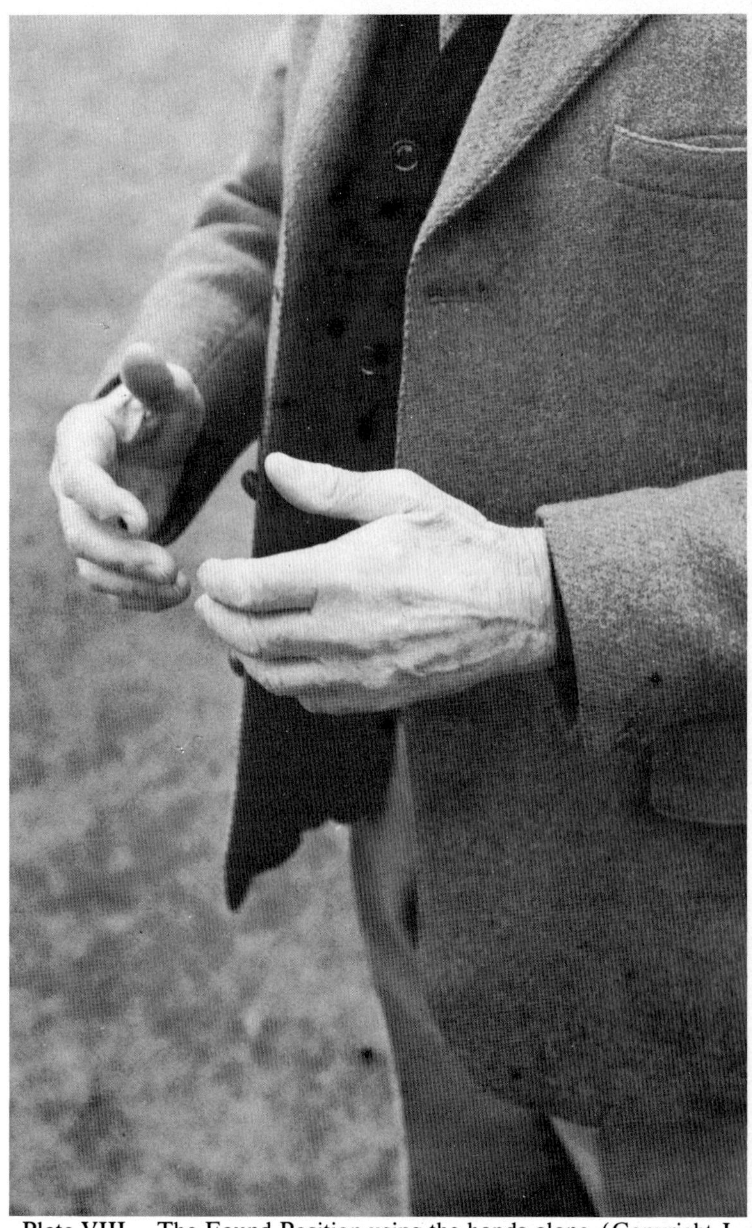

Plate VIII. The Found Position using the hands alone. (Copyright J. A. Muskett)

Plate IX. Swinbrook trial cut. A Post Hole with packing stones still in position.

Plate X. Swinbrook. Part of the main excavation showing stonework and Post Holes.

Plate XI. Walkerdales. Cut 1. Stonework of a floor appearing immediately below the top-soil.

Plate XII. Walkerdales. The Ditch and stonework found in Cut 2.

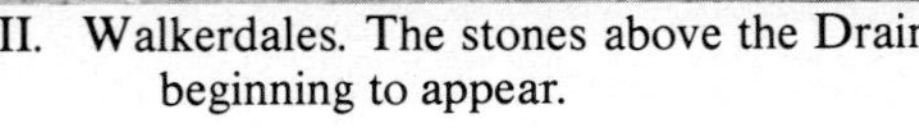

Plate XIII. Walkerdales. The stones above the Drain beginning to appear.

Plate XIV. Walkerdales. A section cut through the Drain shows the stone box type of construction.

Plate XV. Rookwood. The large hole dowsed for and found in Cut 3 which may have held a large stone upright.

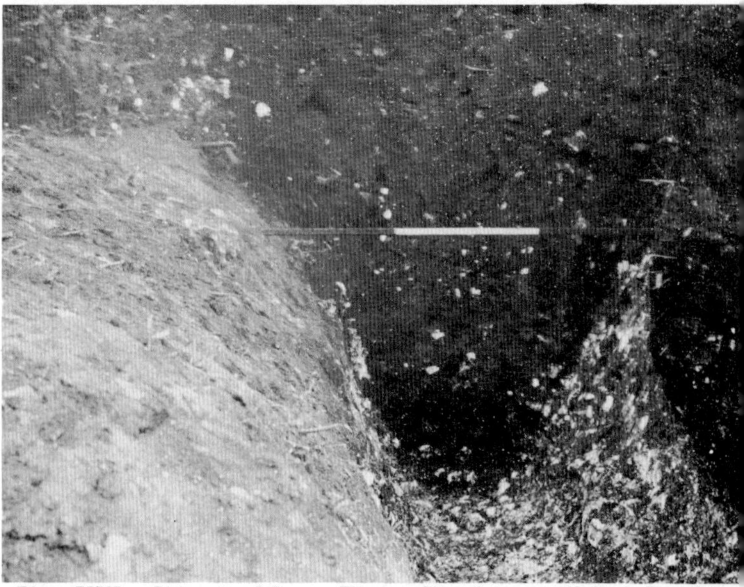

Plate XVI. Chieveley Manor. The profile of the small ditch found in Cut 2.

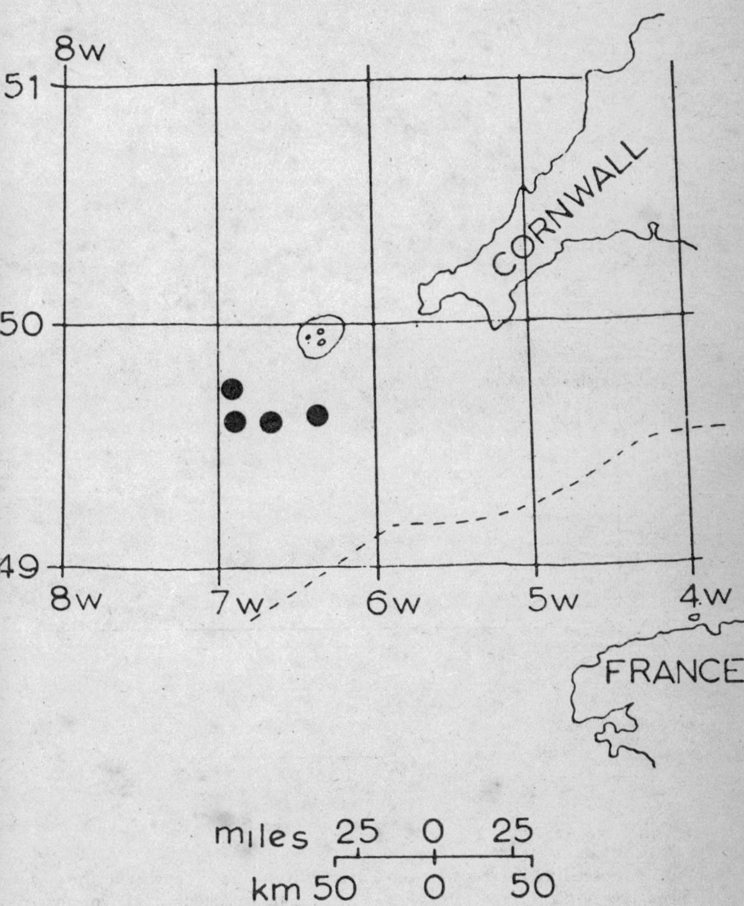

Fig 16 (a).
Four possible oil fields south of the Island of Scilly. Each rated at 6/10.

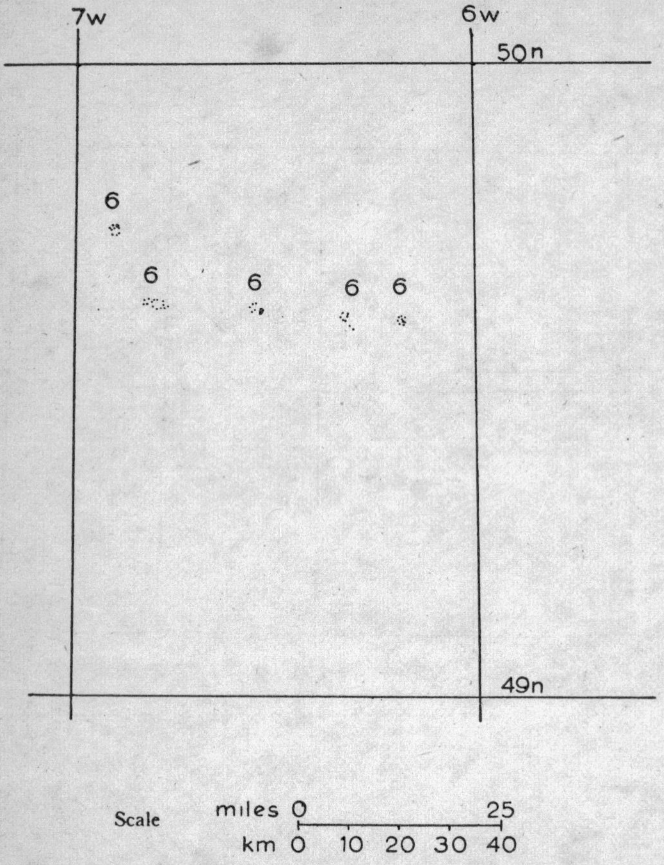

7w
6w
50n
6
6
6
6 6
49n

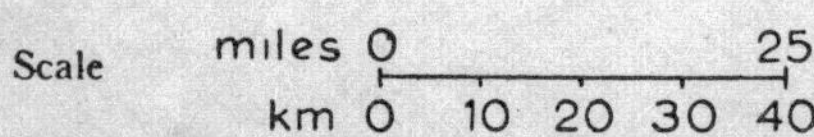

Fig 16 (b).

Area enclosed by 7 degrees west and 6 degrees west, and 49 degrees north and 50 degrees north. This picture is Fig 16 (a) area enlarged four times. Note five good areas of oil. One was overlooked in the map dowsing of Fig 16 (a) due probably to working at the much smaller scale. Each dot is a plotted point. Rate for each oil area is 6/10.

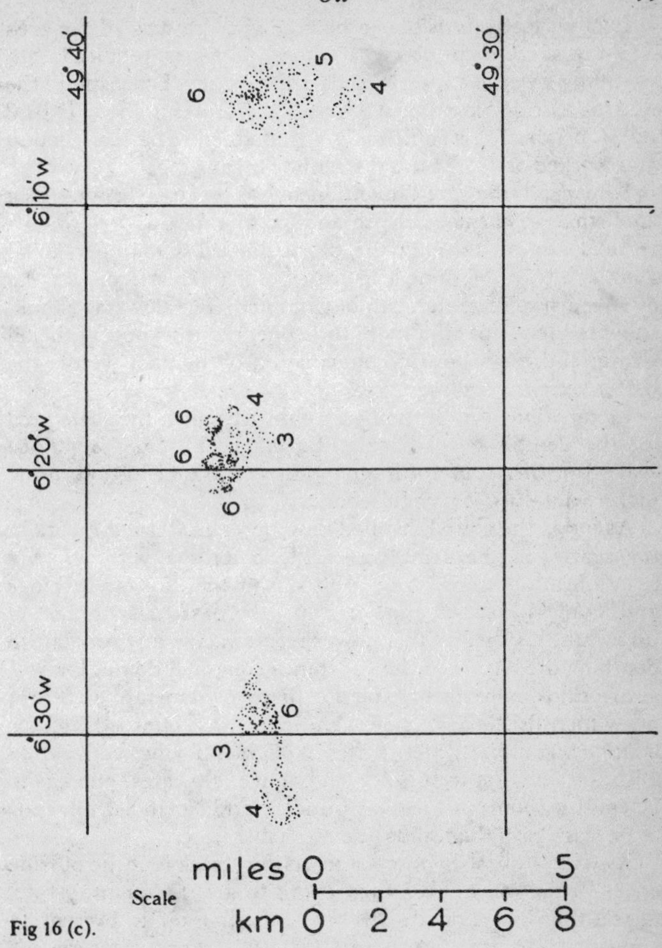

Fig 16 (c).

This shows three of the oil fields re-map dowsed on a scale about four times larger than Fig 16 (b). Dots each mark a plotted point. Figures represent the rate out of 10 for different parts of the fields.

It is perfectly possible to enlarge the drawing of the area again and re-map dowse if more detail is required, but normally I would expect it to be unnecessary. For instance the oil area astride longitude 6 degrees 20 minutes is about 1¾ by 2 miles in size and is sufficiently well defined to be easily found and worked on by the usual scientific means.

So far all the work mentioned has been in Plan. As a confirmation of the oil depth and location it is as well to do a vertical section through the particular oil areas of interest. This is always of value and may be of interest too, as quite often extra information can be obtained. The dowsing should show the levels of oil if more than one, the thickness of the oil strata, and may show in confirmation of the plan picture the better areas for drilling.

As mentioned in Section 4 Distant Dowsing, the scale used for the depthing will have to be different from the surface scale, but this does not matter provided the distortion in the picture obtained is recognised.

As far as the actual detailed dowsing is concerned I work in the search in the same way as I do for many things. My reaction to oil seems to be a bit slower than for other things and, unless careful, one is apt to pass over areas of importance. Whether this slower reaction is in any way due to depth or the nature of the substance sought, I do not know. I suspect it is more likely to be due to my own mental picture of oil which is 'heavy, slow, glutinous' as opposed to, for instance, running water, which is 'light, moving, active' and with the reaction to it quick and active. However, one has to be careful about 'pictures' as I understand North Sea oil tends to be less heavy than some and more like water.

As with a number of other searches, I seek first the outside edges of the oil areas. I then check to get the quantity rate, depth, porosity and re-check to see that oil is present in commercial quantities now. If these are satisfactory the picture is built up by more detailed search within the area, defining by pendulum work those areas more dense in oil. This, as indicated above, may necessitate one or more increases in scale with a re-map dowse for each.

SECTION 9.

Minerals and Precious Stones

As with other fields, the dowser qualified in Minerals and Precious Stones should have no difficulty in locating what he seeks. His main difficulties are:–

First. Identification of the minerals he finds, for he must have some method of checking that he has found what he seeks and not something else.

Second. He must have a means of identification of any mineral he finds whether sought or not.

Third. The establishment of the quantity and quality of the lodes or deposits that he finds.

To solve these problems a number of things are required:–

1. A knowledge of geology in relation to minerals and precious stones is essential. The ideal team is the Geologist and the dowser working together.

2. For identification a dowser has to work out his own method. Most dowsers find that a count or rate can be obtained off any mineral or stone and this seems to be individual to the dowser. The method of establishing these rates is described in Section 3. Counting. The difficulty is acute when a lode or deposit is found and its rate is different from any on the dowser's list. The solution to this is to take geological advice as to what it might be and a trial of possibilities to see if any yield the same rate as the unidentified one. But sometimes the only solution is a trial dig or drill to obtain samples; this is expensive.

3. The establishment of the quantity and the quality is more difficult. Obviously no one is going to do serious work with deposits until samples have been taken, but the dowser

has to be able in his work to differentiate between worthwhile lodes and deposits and others that are not. His geological knowledge may help him in this to a certain extent in computing size, shape, depth and so on, and these can all be obtained by dowsing, but he needs more than this usually and some form of commercial grading is necessary.

For this I use the system of rating out of 10 that I use in many other fields. For me the following ratings in the Mineral and Precious Stones fields give me some guide to the commercial quantity/quality of the lodes and deposits.

9/10 Excellent.
8/10 Excellent.
7/10 Very Good.
6/10 Good
5/10 Average.
4/10 Below average.
3/10 Some available. } Normally not worth extraction.
2/10 Some available. }

These ratings do not take into account the difficulty of extraction or costs of any sort and it is these factors that have to be weighed against the Rating value. For instance a 6/10 rating may in one place be not good enough because of the difficulty of extraction, whereas in another place a rating of 4/10, because of the ease of extraction, may be worthwhile. These ratings are, of course, the dowser's own and if working with a geologist who understands them, they can be used between them but, normally, working with strangers they cannot be used without explanation.

The Search for Minerals. How each mineral usually lies in the ground either in Lodes, Veins, or in Deposit areas must be known to the dowser and it is the edges of these that he will seek initially by dowsing. The whole picture can be established by a mixture of dowsing on plans and on vertical sections of the area. As with other things the search may start on very small scale maps, but eventually quite large plans must be used (see Section 4, Distant Dowsing). As a result of this, the depth below ground of the top and the bottom of the lode etc., the width and thickness and the general area-capacity can be established. (see Fig 12).

The initial work done by distant dowsing in great detail, using varying scales of map and plan can be confirmed by dowsing on the ground to establish the fact of the mineral, to check the lie of the lodes, or the edges of the deposit and to mark spots for test digging or drilling to prove the location and the quality.

In some cases, depending on the type of mineral, inexpensive methods of checking the dowser's forecast can to some extent be used but in the end, drilling is usually necessary.

As with other types of search, much time, money and effort can be saved by the use of qualified dowsers working with the geologist.

The Search for Precious Stones. Here again it is necessary to have some knowledge of the geology affecting each type of stone, how they occur and how they usually lie in the ground.

Basically the method for finding is similar to that for minerals and other subjects, by Map dowsing first on a small scale map or even a rough plan so that a general idea is gained from these. Later, on a larger scale plan, the outside edge of the area of the deposit is marked, then the depth and the quantity/quality rating is obtained. If more detail is required, the area is enlarged again and re-map dowsed, by this means a better idea of the incidence of stones in any particular area can be obtained.

I have only had a little experience in looking for Rubies and for Diamond Pipes. With diamonds the Kimberlite pipe does not seem difficult to locate. With it there usually seems to be a 'wind blown' area running out from the pipe in one direction in which diamonds lie in the ordinary soil. I call these areas wind blown but probably the occurrence is due to weathering mainly by water action of the top of the kimberlite at some time and the distribution of diamonds as it were 'down wind'.

Depths of diamonds and the quantity/quality rate in this 'wind blown' area as well as in the pipe, can be ascertained in the usual dowsing way.

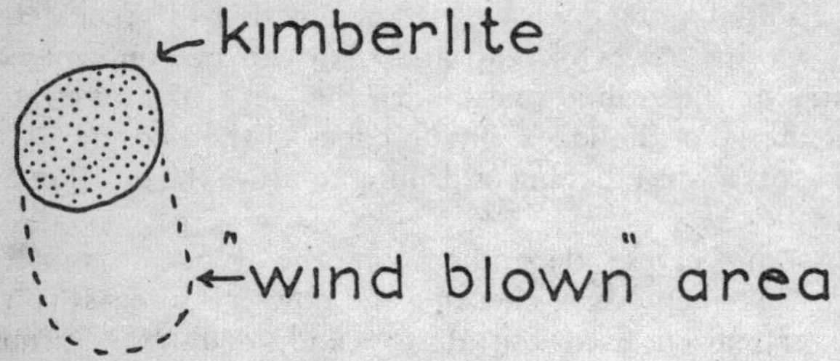

Fig 17. Kimberlite pipe and "wind-blown" area.

SECTION 10.

Pipes. Drains. Cables.

Problems often arise over locating the exact line of the run of pipes, cables and drains, and more often there is difficulty in finding the location of fractures, leaks and blockages in them. Sometimes the cost involved can be considerable. These problems can very often be solved at almost no cost by dowsing means, usually quite simply, though there are times when the pipe or cable or whatever is sought lies close to others similar to it and then there can be difficulties and great care is needed.

The work can be done by distant dowsing and by ground dowsing, which ever is the most suitable, but the normal rules apply and map dowsing should be confirmed on the ground where the trouble is and where local conditions may necessitate very careful work. In all this work, where there is a possibility of mistaking one pipe for another or one cable for another, it is more than ever essential to be able to visualise what is sought and be able to identify the one you seek by some means.

If map dowsing is to be used, and I recommend this first if there is any difficulty at all, plans if available should be used, but quite often these are not available and one has to make do with freehand sketches of a piece of roadway, the garden round the house, a bit of map or an enlargement of a map. These drawings are made to scale as far as is possible, but even a very rough sketch can be useful in giving the approximate location in some cases.

The work can be done also by ground dowsing but this is not always easy and can be very laborious. All sorts of things tend to get in the way, buildings, walls, flower beds, hedges and if a long distance has to be tested it can be very wearisome. Whereas done first by map dowsing most of these difficulties can be overcome or avoided and the location of the pipe or the fault can be located with reasonable accuracy so that the work done by ground dowsing at the end is small and limited to a small area.

When seeking the line of a pipe by map dowsing I use the ordinary method for seeking a linear object. If seeking the location of a blockage, leak or fracture, I get clear in the mind what I am looking for, then allow the pendulum to swing along the line of the pipe. It will do so till it comes over a spot where there is a change in the pipe. This may be due to a junction, perhaps another pipe or something else crossing very close to it, or a fracture or blockage, here it will swing across the line of the pipe. (This is my code). It is then necessary to investigate this spot and find out what is the cause.

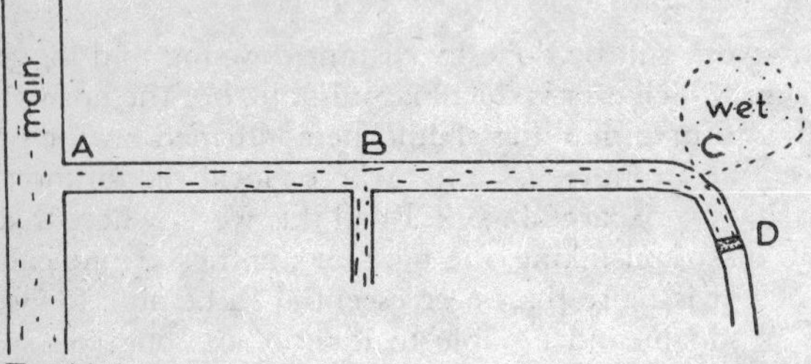

Fig 18. Trouble in a pipe.

Take the case of the search for the block or leak in a pipe that is not delivering water where it should. Check first, as close to the trouble area as possible, that there is water coming into the pipe from the main at A. Then follow the line of the pipe looking for the cause of the trouble. At B the pendulum stops swinging along the pipe and swings across it. I check this to see what is there and find that there is a pipe junction there. I go on searching and reach a spot C where the pendulum swings across the pipe again. On investigation I find that there is a break in the pipe here and for confirmation I find that there is a large area of very wet ground by the fracture point.

It would be tempting to stop there but it is as well to test the rest of the pipe so I continue and find at D another fault which I take to be a blockage as I find no water in the pipe after D.

This method with appropriate variations can be applied to many problems of this sort including the more complicated ones within machines and with electrical subjects.

Using ground dowsing the method is the same in outline but of course is not so easy unless the map dowsing has been already done, then one has a good picture of what the situation is and one is only confirming that this is the case before digging in the right spot to prove the work. The exact spot being found by the ground dowsing.

See Case 2, Owl in Chimney. This was a vertical problem but the same principles apply. Also Case 14, Field Drains.

SECTION 11.

Building Sites.

Much can be done by dowsing to assist Architects and Builders on building sites, both those that are on new and unbuilt-on ground, and those that have been built upon before.

On new ground, a forecast of rock and soil structure can be obtained as well as the line of run, depth and volume of flow of water streams under the site. This information can be shown in plan and by sections across the site.

In places where the site has been built upon before, in addition to the above information, the location of old cellars, wells, large holes, cables, pipes, and old foundations can be shown.

This, like all dowsing, is a somewhat specialised form of work and the technique has to be developed by the dowser himself. Usually the best method will be to do the work by distant dowsing first, and confirming as necessary by work on the ground later. The forecast of rock and soil strata and the location of man-made structures will, of course, have to be proved by drilling or digging.

See Part 3, Case 10, Kidderminster.

SECTION 12

Finding People

I think the finding of people by dowsing is one of the more difficult types of work and I believe this springs from two factors, first the difficulty of identification or differentiation from other people, and secondly from the mobility of the object of search and the inevitable remenance effects of such mobility. Humans, even more than animals, are prone to frequent movement, and it is difficult to re-check the dowsing findings of a person's location when they are frequently on the move. With inanimate objects that lie in the ground, if one locates them 'now' they are unlikely to move, but with humans a 'now' location may be out of date in a few minutes or a few hours. It is noticeable that dowsers have more success over finding dead bodies than in finding living ones, dead bodies do not move on their own, so tend to stay put!

Hence this type of work tends to be fairly specialised and the operator has to be practised at it.

A means of identification is the first essential to work with. The following, in my order of preference, are the means of identification.

Personal knowledge.	If I know the person and can visualize him or her I have no need for a means of identification.
Blood spot.	This lasts for the life of the donor.
Hair sample.	Hair brushes yield useful quantities. (But beware of someone else having used the brush after the owner, this happened to me once).

Finger print	These are not easily come by, but are good.
Writing.	Preferably a signature. I don't like this much as it leads to speculation as to character and may upset the Mind approach.
Clothing.	This must be recently worn by the person, and not handled by others.
Photograph.	I find this of very limited use but better than nothing.

All available information about the person is the next need. Personal habits, customs, way of life, places frequented, last known abode and last sighting. These and the details of the circumstances surrounding the disappearance enable one to get to know the person in some measure, and the more known to one the more is the hope of success in finding but very often little of this can be provided.

Alive or Dead. If this is a factor in the case it should be tested for at this stage as it will affect the method of search.

Maps. The next stage is to get maps and plans that may be of help. If there are any doubts of where the person is likely to be, I go first for a small scale map covering the area of possibility. For example, if the person was thought to be in Scotland but could be in Europe, but not in another continent, I would start on a map of Europe; thereafter the larger the scale of map, the better.

The Search. For simplicity the object of search will be called X. The search at first would be to get a location of where X is 'now'. If accurately done, this would limit him to the Country. One can then go to the map of the country and find the approximate present position.

The next stage is to find out if X is on the move or static. If static, a larger scale map can then be used to get the location in more detail, but in view of the ability to move, the present location must be checked periodically and records kept of apparent positions and times. If in general X appears to centre round a certain spot and only go out for short distances, the problem is nearly solved and has reached the stage when action is needed to get someone to check the found position on the ground.

If, however, X is on the move perhaps by car, air, train or boat, it is necessary to check the position regularly and plot each position and time carefully. From these records will emerge a pattern from which deductions could be made, but it is essential to keep these deductions very general and elastic, as X is a human and able to change his mind and inclinations, none of which the dowser can foresee. It is very important that the dowser, as always, is completely neutral in his search for location and that he is careful to try and locate X 'now'. If he is not neutral, he will tend to try to locate by using the brain and not the Mind. If he does not concentrate on the 'now' location, he may pick up an old position which may date back hours or days.

None of this work is easy, and it is very easy to slip into a fantasy world unless care is taken. In this work, the Need to know is a large factor, just to follow someone is not enough, it has to be really important to know where X is, the more important, the better the work will be.

The method of search with the pendulum is the same as for any other object. When trying to follow somebody or something on the ground with a V rod, the following is my method which really is the same as a directional search for anything.

I first find a point on the route that has been used as if I was picking up the 'scent'. To get the direction of travel I swing the rod across the line of the route from right to left, having the question clearly in mind, it might be 'Which is X's route from here?'; when the rod crosses the line of the route I feel a movement of the rod and this I know indicates the direction. I follow this direction and check from time to time to see if I am on the route. Sometimes the route is easy to follow if X has gone fairly straight and by the obvious way. In these conditions, following can be fairly fast but if the route is a wandering one and devious then following can only be slow as it is important to hang onto the actual track and not lose it, as once lost it may be difficult to pick up again.

If the track is lost I make a cast over the ground in a circle from the last place where I had a successful position check, increasing the diameter of the circle till I pick up the track again.

In this work it is important to keep in mind the possibility of remenance and allow for it if there is any chance that the area of search could have been used by X at some other time. (See Case 18. Following on the ground)

SECTION 13.

Finding Lost Objects.

I find this difficult. I do very little of it, it is at best a side line and I find I am only *really* interested when working for friends or relations, or on some really special case. It is a state of mind one has difficulty in controlling. On the one hand one is professionally keen to succeed and on the other hand when working for friends one seems to be that little bit more in touch with the problem, and that little helps enormously.

I find I don't get more than about 30% success at this, which is low, but it is worth it for the pleasure it gives to those one can help.

As with finding people, I think there are special difficulties. The first is the difficulty of identification. I am thinking of such things as Jewellery, Keys and so on, which are difficult to describe without a photograph, and a coloured one at that. If a photograph or good drawing is available, that is a help. It also helps if I know the owner and the habitat in which the loss has occurred. If I know the owner, I can get the story more clearly and will know what is likely to be fact in the story. Many people find it difficult to remember accurate detail and sometimes even give misleading information quite unintentionally.

The time factor may be of importance. It is possible that a 'scent' 6 months old may make things more difficult to pick up and follow, but this may only be me!

One has to be imaginative and able to cater for happenings that you have not been told about. The way I work is mainly by distant dowsing, and that is a mixture of question and answer and map dowsing.

Having got the story of the loss in as much detail as is possible, I work out on paper the possibilities of where, how, and when in relation to the object. Then I try to find out by dowsing the present position. The process is described in some detail in Section 4 on Distant dowsing in the case of The Brooch.

If the object can be located by Distant dowsing this is satisfactory. If not, then the site may have to be visited and further suitable on-the-spot work done there.

It is difficult enough to locate objects lost which have stayed put when lost, but if they get into other hands, friendly or unfriendly and are moved about, the remenance and movement factors come into it and the search gets more difficult. Under these conditions I suggest working on the problem as if searching for a human as described in Section 12.

For an instance of a Lost Paper see Section 4, Distant Dowsing, and Case 12, The Keys.

SECTION 14

Suiting Soil to Plants.

Using dowsing for suiting soil to plants has great scope in garden work and in farming. It is in practice not difficult, and anyone qualified in dowsing and interested in plants and soil should be able to learn. As with all dowsing, it is necessary to get proof that the work is successful and in this work the proof is neither as quick nor as obvious as it can be in other types of dowsing work. I would advise those who take it up to check their work often to make sure they really are getting results and not imagining it!

The method I use is as follows:–

The simplest case is that of a plant to be put in a certain spot in the garden. I take a handful of soil from where the roots of the plant will be. This is a sample and should be the norm of that bit of the garden.

Place the soil on a clean piece of paper and put on the soil a leaf of the plant to be grown there. If a leaf of that plant is not available, the leaf of a plant of the same kind or even a seed will do.

With in mind that this sample of soil will have a rating in relation to the plant represented by the leaf, find that rating by holding the pendulum over the soil and leaf and start counting. (See Section 3). If, for instance, the initial rating of the relationship of the soil to the plant is 5/10 it is obvious that the soil sample lacks much and will need some additives.

I have a number of obvious additives which are then tried with the soil to see if any will raise the rating of the soil. These are given below, and no doubt there are many others that can be used.

Copper	Zinc	Nitrogen	Phosphate
Iron	Cobalt	Manganese	Bone
Sulphur	Potash	Lime	Salt

Magnesium Sulphate (Epsom Salts)
and some made up fertilisers like
Sequestrine
Phostrogen
Fisons Rose Fertiliser

The additives are represented by the name written on a piece of paper, but if preferred, actual samples can be placed in small envelopes and used instead. As each is selected for trial, it is placed on the soil beside the leaf and the rating taken again. If it helps and the rating has gone up it is left there. If the rating remains the same or goes down, it is removed and the next one tried.

I always record the results of trying each sample as I find otherwise one gets in a muddle if one trusts to memory only. The following is an *example* only of the system of working, it is not an actual case and I have no idea if the sequence of additions would produce the results given.

Example			*Out of 10*
The initial rating for Soil and Leaf			5
Add Phosphate	Take new rating	result	6
Add Nitrogen	,, ,, ,,	,,	8
Add Lime	,, ,, ,,	,,	6
as Lime has reduced the rating remove it. Hence rating still			8
Add Epsom Salts	Take new rating	result	9
Add Iron	,, ,, ,,	,,	9
as Iron has not raised the rating remove it. Rating still			9
Add Bone	Take new rating	result	10

It would be possible to try out other additives to see if a simpler solution using fewer additives is available, for instance Phostrogen or some other produce might reduce the number.

The next stage is to discover the quantity of each additive required. Gardening experience will guide many people, but in most cases very small quantities will be required over the area, and a quantity such as a number of pinches per square foot or square yard would be sufficient. These amounts can be ascertained by dowsing if required.

If a large area of garden is to be cropped it may be necessary to take samples of soil from more than one part if it is suspected that there are soil changes.

This system can also be applied to larger areas such as fields, but usually it is simpler to rate such large areas by Distant dowsing. If the soil of a field is similar all over, a rate taken at several places in the field will show this, and treatment of the field can be the same all over. If, however, the rate for parts of the field varies, then the additive treatment for each will have to be worked out. If the ideal solution is complicated, then a compromise may have to be used to meet practical farming considerations.

To rate a field I use a plan or drawing of it to the scale I need and test parts of it with the leaf or seed of the crop on it as if it was the soil sample described above.

For deciding the quantity per acre required of each additive, the same procedure is followed, except that the drawing of the field is used instead of the soil sample.

SECTION 15.

Elementary Self Teaching. Qualifications. Tests. Standards.

Elementary Self Teaching.

Most of this book is aimed at helping the novice to teach himself, but the following outline may help with the organisation of his self teaching.

First re-read the basic rules given in Section 1, these give a background to work from and an aim.

Learn to use the pendulum with accuracy, and learn to use the Mind in your search work, once you can do this you are on your way.

Once the pendulum work indoors has been learnt, outdoor work becomes easier. There the same sensitivity is being used in another atmosphere and perhaps with other tools, but the basic thoughts, ideas and mind work is the same.

In learning the pendulum work start with finding the Yes and the No, then practice on the exercises given below. They are only exercises and should be dropped as soon as possible and not persisted with. Go on to the practical work inside and outside as soon as possible, for instance some of the drawings in Part III could be utilised if traced off on to paper as there is quite a lot underground not shown in the drawings. Drains and cables round houses, the line of pipes underground, and maps that show wells, can all be worked upon for practice and the results can be checked for correctness.

Try out for yourself all that is claimed that can be done by dowsing and see if it can be made to work for you.

Find out what applications of dowsing interest you and start using it for these in a practical way. The 'need to know' is a great help, it seems to sharpen up one's sensing ability!

Some exercises.

These are elementary and are suggested only as a means of developing the use of the Mind in the early stages.

(a) Try over an electric light cable – a standard lamp flex is useful. Use the pendulum to find out if the cable is Live or Not. By this you can establish what is your Yes or your No.

(b) Put four similar coins and one different, under a cloth, move them around and then seek the different one.

(c) Take five or more black playing cards and one red one, shuffle and lay them face down on the table and seek the red one.

(d) Take three or more cups and put water or a coin in one. Cover them up, move them around and then seek the one with the coin or the water.

(e) Fill a large but shallow box with sand. Place a metal object in it and shake up the box so that the object can move its position. Seek its position.

(f) Get someone to hide a note or object in the shelf of a bookcase. Work along the bookcase with a pendulum to locate it. A rod can be used for this also.

(g) Get someone to take a leaf from a hedge or a plant. Take the leaf in your hand and find the plant from which the leaf came.

(h) Work over your own house to find the run of the drains, electric cables, water pipes, gas pipes etc., both inside and outside, then if you want more practice try your friend's pipes and drains!

There are many variants of the above that you can think up if you wish to develop your seeking sensitivity – but remember you must use the Mind and Not the Brain or the five physical senses. The trained dowser 'knows' the answer to his question subconsciously. He uses his tools as visual indicators of what he knows in his mind. If he uses samples they are mind focussers.

Keep your dowsing as simple and as natural as you can.

Qualifications, Tests, Standards.

There are often four stages in a dowser's career, so be warned!

Stage 1. Keen to learn. Takes a lot of trouble. Gets on well.

Stage 2. Becoming confident. Gets so confident that he thinks that all can be done by dowsing and he can do it! During this period he may have some remarkable successes. He may even go into print!

Stage 3. He gets over confident, careless and the discipline of the mind tends to slip. He makes a lot of mistakes: (hence the value of work where the correctness of it is demonstrable). He is brought up sharply and if he is wise, he takes a look at himself and his work. If he does this and goes on to quiet, careful work with a humble outlook, acknowledging that what he has is a gift, then he may reach –

Stage 4. where he will develop and expand his dowsing with experience and do really good and useful work.

Ideally it would be nice to have standard qualifications for dowsers so that their ability was known. At present I do not think we can do more than judge ability other than by successful results, and this is not always easy to assess.

Tests for dowsers seldom work and, more often than not, end in failure. The reason for this lies, I think, in the root of the dowsing ability. Those that set up the tests invariably wish the dowser to demonstrate that dowsing works or that he can do it. He is then faced with a 'parlour trick' where there is no real 'need' to find or to find out something, and he is really only showing how clever he is! Under these conditions the mind machinery doesn't work properly and he fails.

So, for the present, with our very inadequate knowledge of

how dowsing works, I do not think we can do more than urge that we expect from the qualified dowser an outlook that expects nothing short of success – not boastfully but humbly – based on a quiet acceptance of an ability gifted to him, but developed by his own hard work and trained in the harsh field of experience, where success and failure mean much to his professional integrity.

PART 3.

Job Instances.

This part consists of accounts of some jobs I have done. To the novice I hope all will be of interest, some instructive and some cautionary! The selection is broadly based so that the width and scope of the use of dowsing is well illustrated.

The only obvious omission is that of water-finding, but this has never been one of my fields. Novices who wish to specialize in that field can find plenty of advisers.

CASE 1.

The Wishing Well Overflow.

This case has a special place in my memory for it is the first useful job of work I carried out by dowsing. It was not an easy one and the answer to the problem was far from what was expected. The successful result of this case gave me just the confidence I needed to get going in a new type of work which at that time was regarded by my family and others as, if nothing worse, a bit odd!

At my old home in Dumfriesshire there was a half-moon shaped concrete ornamental basin called the Wishing Well about 12 ft in diameter, it lay half way up the hill behind the house and to the southward of it. This was filled all the year round by a spring that flowed out of the rock. There was an overflow system, the rose of which stood a bit off centre near the middle, but the system had not worked for many years and no-one knew where it led to. It was assumed that it led down

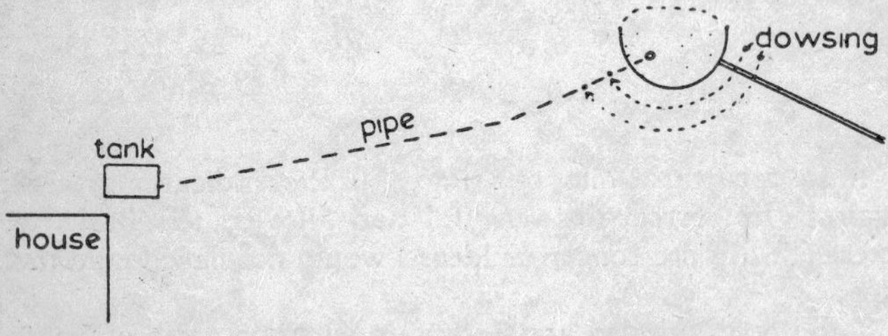

Fig 19. The Wishing Well overflow pipe.

the hill somewhere to the South West. To get rid of the overflow water a cut had been made in the wall of the basin at the SW and the water ran down the hill in an improvised ditch and tended to make an awful mess at times when the overflow was heavy.

So I decided to try out my dowsing to see if I could find the run of the blocked pipe and perhaps clear it.

As I thought that the pipe probably ran to the SW, I hunted for a lead pipe in that area first, but found nothing. I then walked round the edge of the basin from South towards North. When I got close to the bank at the Northern end, the rod turned, so I marked the spot with a peg. I cannot say I was optimistic as this was, I thought, just the wrong way for the overflow pipe to run. However, I tried again on an arc further out from the basin and again at the NW the rod turned. I pegged this spot too and, while doing so, noticed that the two pegs and the rose of the overflow were in a straight line. So I thought that possibly I had found the pipe. A little spade work at each peg revealed at 18 inches down a lead pipe running in the general line of the rose and the two pegs! I had found the overflow pipe, but where on earth did it go to?

By dowsing I followed the pipe down the hill to the NW and confirmed that it was there by digging in places. Finally I found that the pipe ran into an underground tank that no-one knew about just behind the house and was a relic of the days before mains water. I had known of a well of water under what was known as the pump room at the other end of the house, but this was obviously another additional supply which lay just outside the kitchen.

Notes.

1. Be neutral while dowsing. All the indications were against the correct answer. If I had allowed the Brain to interfere with pre-conceived ideas I would not have found the pipe.

2. Be open minded and persistent when on a job of work. The answer is there somewhere.

CASE 2.

The Owl in the Chimney.

In my old home the kitchen was up against an outside wall that was built of sandstone and the flue from the Esse cooker went up inside the wall in a long dog-leg to the chimney on the roof. I knew approximately how it ran as there was an inspection box half way up at the dog-leg.

The chimney had been swept fairly recently so when one day the Esse began to play up and wouldn't draw, I thought there must be a blockage of some sort in the flue.

So I drew a picture of the flue from the Esse via the dog-leg up to the top of the chimney, more or less to scale and map dowsed it. I got signs of a blockage at a point some 4 ft above the elbow in the flue. I tried this area by ground dowsing by getting up a ladder and trying round the area with a pendulum, and was able to pinpoint, as I thought, the point of blockage.

The local builder was a friend of mine so he came along and took out a stone where I told him to. Having done so he found that the correct stone had been removed and the flue was exposed. He then put his arm into the flue, fiddled about for a moment and then produced the dead body of an Owl!

Notes. Many unlikely problems can be solved by dowsing. Be ingenious in the use of your ability. The flue was vertical, but it was easy to map dowse as if horizontal. Vertical dowsing is exactly the same as horizontal, provided the mental approach is correct.

CASE 3.

Return from Suez.

At the time of the British Operations at Suez in 1957, my son was serving with a Brigade Headquarters out there. At home we knew by the news media that the troops were being withdrawn about the 23rd December, but we had no means of knowing when he was leaving nor in what ship.

It was in my very early days as a dowser, and I thought that it would be interesting to try to plot his progress back through the Mediterranean.

I found an old scarf of his that I used as a means of identification of him among the large number of men he would be with.

For a number of nights I plotted his position each evening at 6 pm on a small scale atlas which had the whole Mediterranean on one page. These positions were converted to Latitude and Longitude.

Eventually I got a letter from him posted at Gibraltar which told me the ship's name and when they expected to get to Southampton.

Before the date of arrival I wrote to the Captain of the ship and gave him the first four plots. I heard nothing for a little time but eventually I did get a letter to say that he had had the ship's position for my times worked out and that the errors were as follows:—

24 Dec	Lat. correct	Long. correct
25 Dec	Lat. correct	Long. 1 degree out
26 Dec.	Lat. correct	Long. 52 minutes out
27 Dec	Lat. correct	Long. 3 degrees out

Notes. The accuracy of these four plots seems good to me taking into account the scale of map being used and the amateur state of the dowser! [But see below.]

Tracing people is difficult and requires much practice.

If the person being traced is well known to the operator no sample is necessary. But if not known, a sample of some kind is essential. (See Section 12, Finding People).

As is often the case the first bit of work is the more accurate. Later one may get slipshod and over-confident and think it is easy – it is then that mistakes occur, as they did here in the longitude.

CASE 4.

Swinbrook.

I was told by a friend who lived at Swinbrook Cottage that she thought that there might be an archaeological site under the garden.

I did not know the garden, so one day went to see it. Nothing showed on the surface and it looked a most unlikely location for an old site as it was down in the flood plain of the river Windrush which sometimes floods even today, and must have done so more often in days gone by. There was also better building ground not far away.

During this visit I did no dowsing work as I prefer to do the map dowse first, but I took away with me a portion of the 1/2500 map which I enlarged to a multiplication of 4.

Much to my surprise when map dowsed this showed a rectangular site some 35 ft by 60 ft. At first I didn't believe it for at this stage in the work all sorts of things can lead one astray, particularly near houses and in a village as this was. Drainage ditches and ditches of all sorts carrying pipes and cables and trenches of all sorts can be pit-falls for the unwary.

However, I went to the house again and did my ground dowsing and sure enough the same picture emerged as in the map dowse, so I decided that there might be a site there.

I dated it by dowsing and got a figure of AD 1125.

The owner was keen to dig up the lawn under which the site lay, so a little time later we put down a trial cut of 10 by 4 ft across what seemed to me to be the outside edge of the site. In the cut we very quickly began to find medieval pottery and animal bones both in largish quantities for a cut of this small size. Later we found two post holes which finally clinched the fact that we had a lived-on site.

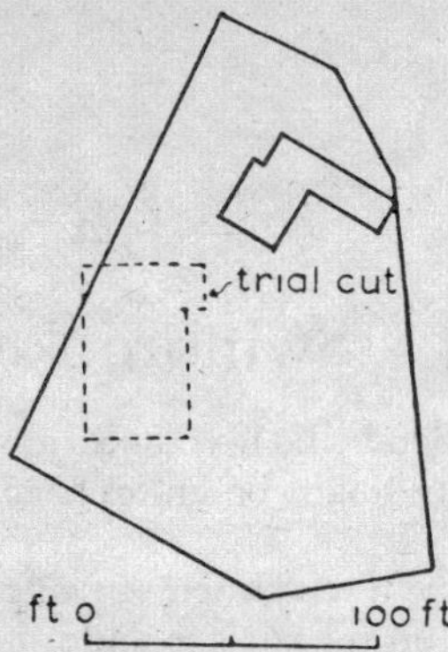

Fig 20. Swinbrook. The dotted line shows the outline of the site as originally dowsed.

Later in the year we carried out a partial excavation of the site and found five floors, part of two walls, many post holes and a large quantity of pottery and other artifacts (see Plate IX and X). When the pottery was examined it was identified as mainly 11th century with a little 12th century, so the date obtained by dowsing before excavation was accurate enough.

Notes. Trust your dowsing, but check and re-check by various means. It is nearly always better to do the map dowsing before dowsing on the ground. Geographically it is much easier – for instance flower beds don't obstruct, working out and recording detail is easier and it is much quicker.

The date obtained by dowsing from a complex site, as this was, will usually be that of the latest occupation.

CASE 5.

A Novice Tries.

I was helping with the excavation of the Roman Fort of Broomholm in Dumfriesshire both as a worker and as a dowser.

One afternoon I was trying to trace the line of one of the defensive ditches with my rod when a friend of mine appeared. He was Chairman of a well known local paper and wanted to know what we were doing and in particular he was interested in what I was doing.

I told him what I was engaged in and asked him if he would like to try. He said he would, so I gave him my rod and showed him how to use it. Having explained what he should think about I set him off across the line of where I thought the line of the defensive ditch ran. Nothing showed on the surface.

Shortly the rod turned in his hand but he said not to count that as he had made it turn by mistake. So I set him off again on another line over the ditch, but I marked his spot when he was not looking. Shortly afterwards the same thing happened again and again he said he had made the rod turn. Again I set him off over the line of the ditch at an angle so that he could not see the two markers I had put in the ground at his two previous dowsed points. A third time the rod turned in his hand and I marked the spot.

He gave up arguing when I showed him that the three spots where the rod had turned were in a straight line and were where I thought the ditch ran. He was a bit shaken when he realised that he could do this thing that he did not believe in.

A number of years later he accepted that he was a natural dowser and joined the British Society of Dowsers.

Notes. He was a natural dowser but at first could not accept this 'peculiar' thing. This applies to quite a lot of people.

CASE 6.

A Lost Stone.

I was having supper with a friend, a simple affair in the kitchen, there was a bottle of wine and the atmosphere was very relaxed.

She began to tell me of a pear-shaped blue stone that had been of sentimental value that had disappeared a year or more ago when she had moved from a flat to this house, and she was beginning to think that it had been stolen.

'But it is in this house' I found myself saying. I suppose I had become interested and had 'switched on'. I was told that it was not possible as search had often been made. However, I maintained that I thought it was in the house and suggested she took me round the house mentally, since I did not know it well.

So I was taken mentally to each room. The rooms on the ground floor were all negative. On the next floor they were all negative till we came to her bedroom, this was positive.

She then mentioned each piece of furniture in turn, these were all negative till the dressing-table which was positive. It was described to me as a knee-hole table with four drawers on the left, four on the right and one in the centre. The drawers on the left were negative, as was the centre one. But the drawers on the right were positive. We went down the drawers on the right in turn and I said it was in the second. I was told that that drawer had often been searched and that it could not be there. So the matter rested there. Next day however, the drawers on the right side were searched. The second, which I had said it was in contained no blue stone, but the one immediately under it did produce the stone tidily done up in a brown envelope! I had been four inches out in my depthing!

Notes. An example of the use of the Mind and no tools.

Allowing the Mind to work.

Confidence in the ability to do it with just the Mind, undoubtedly the relaxed atmosphere helped.

A system not recommended for really serious work unless the operator is skilled and practised in this type of work.

For the Method used see Section 3, Using the Tools. Mind alone.

CASE 7.
Walkerdales.

This story is included because it was in part a dowsing success and, in part, a failure and serves to emphasise the need for care in all parts of the dowsing work prior to trial excavation.

We had for some time been seeking proof of a permanent Roman occupation of Banffshire inland from the coast for about 8 miles in the general area of Banff-Portsoy-Buckie. One of the means of proof would have been the finding of a Roman Signal Station on a route. By map dowsing I thought that I had found such a signal station in a field at Walkerdales Farm.

In 1973 I seemed to get confirmation of the map dowsing although the ground dowsing was never altogether satisfactory and there seemed to be signs of other man-made structures on the site. Unfortunately, for one reason and another, the ground dowsing on the site had to be more hurried than I like, and I was unable to spend the time on it that is really necessary and, in due course, I paid the penalty.

Nothing showed on the surface of the field and there was no tradition of anything in the vicinity.

In June, with the kind permission of the farmer we put down two large trial cuts, both placed by dowsing and, in both cases, came down immediately on man-made structures. (Fig 21. Cuts 1 and 2). To this extent the dowsing was extremely successful, but as we went on with the excavation it became clear that we had not got Roman structures but those which might be Medieval judging by their shape.

In fact what we had found is of considerable interest but it did not further our studies of the Roman situation, and this was a severe disappointment.

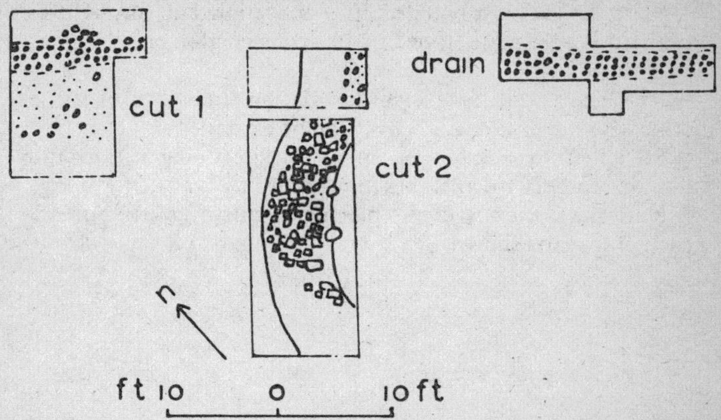

Fig 21. Part of the excavation at Walkerdales Farm showing Cuts 1 and 2 and the Cut over the Drain.

I think one of the causes of the mistake was in dating incorrectly the curved structure shown in cut 2, which could have been mistaken by shape for the outside edge of a signal station to which it is similar.

Plate XI shows the stone work we came down to in cut 1.

Plate XII shows the ditch and the stone work in it found in cut 2.

As there seemed to be a linear structure along the northern edge of cut 1 we tried by dowsing to see if it continued to the NE above cut 2. By dowsing it seemed to do so and we put a cut over a length of it as shown in Fig 21. When excavated, the accuracy of the dowsing was demonstrated by what can be seen in Plate XIII which is a photograph of the excavation of this cut at the time when the stonework over the drain was beginning to appear.

It will be noticed that the drain does not run accurately down the length of the cut, the reason for this is that the cut is laid square to the grid of the site, but despite this we have been able to get a good length of the drain accurately into a narrow cut thanks to being able to plot the position of the drain by dowsing.

Plate XIV is a photograph of a section cut through the drain, this shows the stone box-like construction of it.

Notes. The need for accurate dating before excavation, otherwise much time and effort can be wasted.

Sufficient time must be spent on site doing the ground dowsing, otherwise mistakes may occur.

Note the accuracy of the placing of cuts over structures in each of the cuts shown.

CASE 8.

Gledenholm.

Early in 1966 I was searching a part of the hill country of Dumfriesshire for Bronze Age living sites which might be connected with similar period grave sites we had recently found in that area. By map dowsing I found what I thought might be three such Bronze Age living sites. At that time little was known about the size, shape and layout of sites of that period in Scotland so I had not much to go on except the date.

When I got to the ground for the ground dowsing I found the site areas very suitable for living sites and the ground dowsing seemed to confirm the map dowsing, so I selected one of the sites for a trial excavation.

The trial cut over the edge of this site was not immediately successful in that although I was fairly sure I had found a floor there was no immediate proof of a site so I decided to put a cut over the edge of the one next door.

This produced immediate results in that I uncovered the top of a pallisade trench and post holes. Having got definite proof of a site I used map dowsing and ground dowsing as I went on with the excavation. I see in my notes of the excavation that on 27 July I tried out three of my young girl helpers with the V rod over the edge of where I thought there was the edge of a hut and in each case the rod turned for them at approximately the right spot and I have added 'They were thrilled'. Also on a later date two professional archaeological friends of mine came to see the site and were tried out with the V rod over the edge of the same hut and the rod turned for both. I see I have noted that '... they were flabbergasted, I was pleased!' One of them now accepts the value of dowsing but

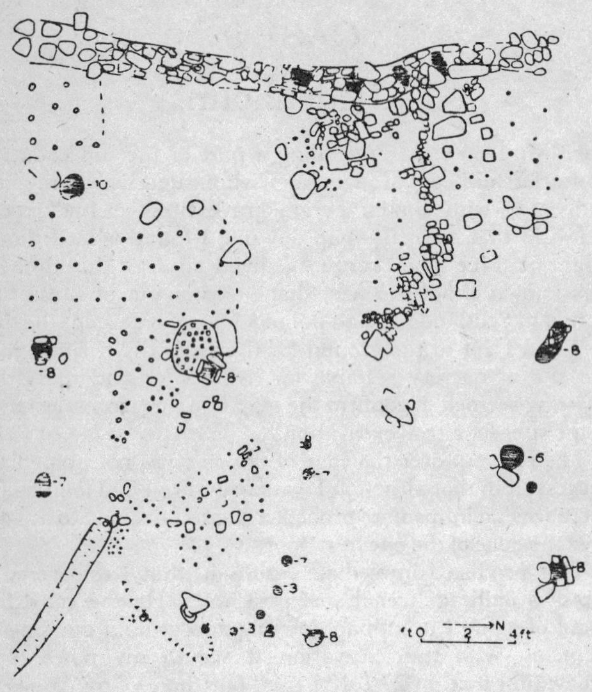

Fig 22. A plan drawing of part of the Gledenholm excavation. This shows some of the pallisade trench with Post Holes in it, some Post Holes of the interior, and part of a Drip Trench which ran under the eaves of a hut roof.

neither has to my knowledge ever made use of it in his work!

The pallisade trench was large and stone packed but some post holes were clearly visible in it. At the bottom of the trench fortunately there was a large quantity of carbonised wood, the residue presumably of the pallisade being burnt. This when tested to find the radio-carbon age was dated at BC 1010 (plus or minus 90). This date in Scotland is accepted as the late Bronze age.

Fig 22 shows a small part of the excavated site. Unfortunately I was never able to complete the excavation as I moved to another part of the country.

The site is on level ground and although only a short distance below the surface of the ground nothing recognisable shows on the surface. It lies in the foot-hill country and is in no way remarkable from the location point of view so is unlikely ever to have been found without dowsing. While the site itself has been preserved for further work the ground around has now been planted with forest.

CASE 9.

Rookwood.

In 1974 I was invited to examine a field called Rookwood near Petersfield. It had been thought that there might be an ancient archaeological site in the field and pottery had been found, but nothing showed on the surface of the ground and there was no tradition locally of anything there.

The subsoil is Sandstone (Greensand) with a covering of about six inches of soil. The field is wedge shaped about 400 yards long and 160 yards at the widest part.

From the map dowsing I found what I thought was the remains of a large monument consisting of an outer circle of large stones with two smaller circles within it. In addition there were signs of Iron Age and Roman structures.

The ground dowsing seemed to confirm this somewhat complex and difficult site, so arrangements were made to put down three trial cuts to try to prove the fact of an archaeological site and if possible to demonstrate the fact of a Henge.

Cut Number 1. This was intended to be across what I thought was a shallow ditch which seemed to mark the outer edge of the Monument and in which I thought the holes for the large stones had been cut. The cut was 10 feet by 3 feet because we were short of time and labour, so I could not make the cuts as large as I would have liked. This cut produced a trench holding a lead pipe which carried water to an animal trough in the field and I was told that prior to this the run of the pipe had not been known to the farmer! It also produced the expected rock-cut ditch lying across the lie of my cut. It was 5 feet wide at the top and 2 feet deep. (Fig 23 (a)).

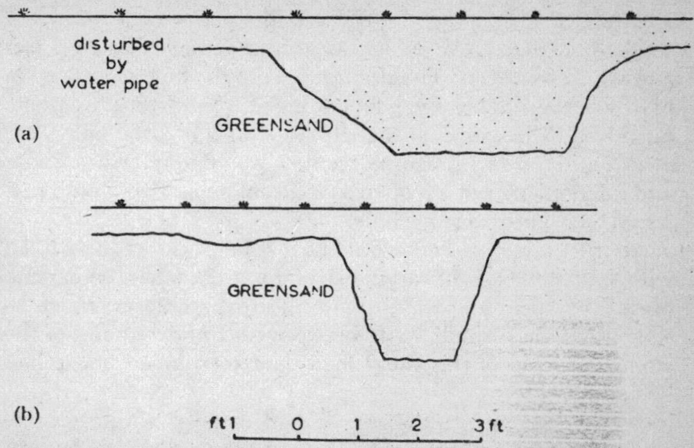

Fig 23. (a) Cut 1. Profile of rock-cut ditch in west baulk of the cut.
(b) Cut 2. Profile of rock-cut ditch showing in the west baulk of the cut.

Cut Number 2. This was intended to be over the same outer ditch some little distance to the west. It was 8 feet by 3 feet and came down across another rock-cut ditch which ran across it (Fig 23(b)) which was 3 feet wide at the top and 2 feet 6 inches deep. So this cut was accurately placed over a small ditch but I suspect that this is not the outer edge of the Henge but a ditch which may be something to do with the Iron Age period.

Cut Number 3. This was right out in the middle of the field and was intended to be over one of the large stone holes in which had stood originally one of the big stones of the outer circle.

The Cut was 10 feet by 10 feet in area. When the top soil was removed we came down on a man-made floor of clay and sandstone chips mixed. At first I thought that I had made a mistake and that there was no stone hole, but the dowsing continued to show a large hole under the floor so we recorded the floor and went on down through it. It was in fact 9 inches thick.

Under the floor we found a large man-cut hole in the sandstone (plate XV) which measured some 7 feet by 3 feet and was 3 feet deep. The deepest part of the hole measured in plan 2 feet 6 inches by 1 foot 6 inches. Sandstone weathers quickly but the edges of the cut stone in this large hole were not weathered so I presume the hole was made for a purpose and filled in and not left open as a casual hole. This would fit if it had been cut as a stone hole.

After this hole had gone out of use it had been crudely filled with sandstone bits of varying sizes up to 12 inches, which had been pitched in any way just to fill up the hole, so much so that there were small voids between and under many of the stones. On top of this the 9 inch floor mentioned above had been built.

So here again by dowsing we had come down accurately on to what we had expected and the planned size of our cut fitted well the size of the hole found.

I had hoped to have a further season on the site during which I had intended to find and excavate three consecutive large stone holes belonging to the outer ring of the site and thus I hoped to prove its existence. Unfortunately due to the sale of the property this, as yet, has not been possible.

One of the difficulties of dealing with this period of site is that archaeologically little is known of their detailed layout. The other difficulty is that this is a complex site having possibly two other periods on top of the older one and this makes it difficult initially to disentangle by dowsing one period from another before any excavation is done. Once the trial cuts are successfully made it then becomes much easier as then there are known and proved features from which to work.

In this case we now have two man-made rock-cut ditches to work from if required and also one large man-made rock-cut hole from which to work in search for proof of a Henge.

The dowsing was accurate in that each trial cut did produce the type of object sought. With hind sight one often feels one could have done better and placed the cuts with more advantage but if one gets three out of three correct on a completely unknown area one is not doing too badly!

CASE 10.

Kidderminster.

In 1968 the centre of Kidderminster had been demolished and plans for the rebuilding were about to be put into practice. The firm doing the work had heard that there had been numerous wells dug in the old days in that area. The subsoil is a soft sandstone, and the danger was that new foundations placed over one of the wells might be affected in time.

I was asked to find out if there were any old wells and locate them by dowsing. I searched the area by map dowsing and found what appeared to be several wells and some cavities. When I got to the site it was covered with large heaps of sand and earth, piles of building material and bulldozers, and it was quite a job trying to work among it all, much less locate the spots where with the map dowsing I had found possible well locations.

In the end we did find and prove two well locations and one large pit, presumably a rubbish pit that was very large and deep. Such others that I thought were there did not affect the buildings, and were ignored.

Note. See Section 3. Using the Tools. Working among the turmoil of a site is not difficult.

CASE 11.

Chieveley Manor.

I was asked by the owner of Chieveley Manor to examine by dowsing the Church which lies by the house, to see which parts of the building were old. While doing this by map dowsing, I searched the churchyard and found what appeared to be a track that ran through the churchyard and into the walled garden of the Manor. So then I map dowsed the area of the Manor, garden and orchard and found what appeared to be a complex site with several periods present. These periods I tried to outline and date. Parts showed clearly but other parts were confused. The periods represented seemed to date by dowsing as follows:–

Iron Age about BC 50
Roman Age about AD 80
Saxon Age about AD 850

A visit to the Manor and work by dowsing on the ground confirmed that there seemed to be a complex site there and I was able to pick up and locate certain features that fitted in with the map dowsing.

The owner was interested and allowed me to select a spot for a trial cut in the orchard where it could do no harm and was out of sight from the house. I selected this spot because I thought there was a large defensive ditch there. I dowsed for the accurate position of the near and far edge of the ditch and marked out the cut to be at right angles to the line of the ditch.

When we excavated we found the cut had been well placed and within it was a large defensive ditch 12 ft wide and 5 ft 6 inches deep. The ditch was clay lined. Had I known at that time that there was chalk behind the clay I would have gone

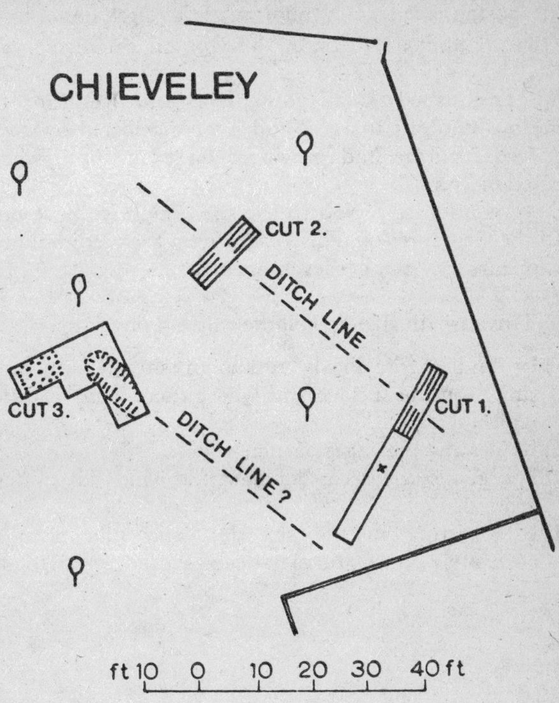

Fig 24. The trial cuts at Chieveley.

through it and found it was similar in construction to the one in Cut 2 mentioned below.

An extension to this original cut, but only 18" deep disclosed a considerable quantity of Carbonised wood. A sample of this was dated by radio carbon means and a date of AD 808 ± 80 was given.

Thus, with this first trial excavation we had established the fact of a large defensive ditch, later to be confirmed as probab.y Roman Punic of the 1st century AD, and an activity date that confirmed the fact that there was a Saxon period to the site.

Cut 2 established a continuation of the ditch found in Cut 1 and here it appears to be of the Roman Punic type which dates at 1st century AD.

Cut 3 established a smaller outer ditch and an entrance.

The position of Cuts 1, 2 and 3 were selected by dowsing and were accurate and provided, on excavation, what we expected to find.

There is another period to the site which we have not yet found the structures of. This is shown by the medieval pottery that appears in the upper levels of each cut.

Notes. This case illustrates well the value of dowsing:–

(a) In finding previously unknown sites where nothing shows on the surface and where there is no tradition of anything.
(b) In locating the edges of such a site.
(c) For giving a forecast of date for what lies under the ground.
(d) In assisting in the selection and placing of cuts accurately over features to be excavated.

CASE 12.

The Keys.

A friend telephoned one morning to say that she had beer away on holiday and had returned the evening before and now couldn't remember where she had hidden the keys of the picture gallery where she works, before she left for the holiday. She said that they must be either in the gallery or in her flat and to find them was urgent.

I knew the gallery and part of the flat, but asked her to describe the flat in detail while I drew the plan of it on a piece of paper.

After doing a little work on the problem I telephoned and suggested she searched the top left hand drawer of her desk in the gallery. While I held on she did that and eventually said 'No, there are keys there, but those are some spare keys of the flat'.

So I went back to work and map dowsed the flat. Later I telephoned again and said there were three places in the flat that she could search.

1. Behind the books on a bookshelf some three feet left of the fireplace in the living room.
2. In the right hand drawer of the work top in the kitchen.
3. In the long hanging cupboard in the bedroom, five feet from the end away from the door.

That evening she telephoned to say:–

1. Was in fact a place where she did occasionally hide things, but the keys were not there.
2. In the right hand drawer of the work top in the kitchen

she had found two long lost spare keys of the front door of the flat, but the missing keys were not there.

3. In the long hanging clothes cupboard, just where I had said, she found a basket hanging on the wall behind the clothes, and in the basket were the missing keys.

This is quite an interesting story. In this case those who are expert at this sort of work may say that I had four shots at location before I got the right one. This is true, but perhaps if I had been able to visualise the particular keys in detail I might not have got mixed up with the other two lots. But the fact that three sets of keys were found is to me remarkable. However, it does point the lesson that when there are many similar to what is sought, some means of identification is needed to enable one to distinguish the right one.

The time factor has to be considered too. 'Where are XX keys now?' is the sort of question that should be asked. I have no doubt that the gallery keys may have been in the top left hand drawer of the desk quite often, but they were not there when I was searching.

CASE 13.

Daviot.

In 1975 the owner of the House of Daviot asked me to examine by dowsing the ground North of the present house to see if I could find any traces of a castle which from the family records was said to have stood there or somewhere near. It was thought probable that the stone from it would have been robbed for the construction of other later buildings round about, hence little would remain.

The ground to the north of the present house forms a level-topped promontory which projects into the valley and forms an ideal position for a defended site as the ground falls away very steeply on three sides, and the only easy access is from the South or South West.

Map dowsing seemed to show the possibility of more than one site of differing periods, among them parts of a stone built building which by dowsing dated at about AD 1440.

When I went there the ground dowsing seemed to confirm the map dowsing in parts and particularly on the southern edge of the possible stone building.

To get confirmation of a site we put down a cut along the line of where I thought a wall foot ran, and Fig 25 shows part of the result. This original cut was intended to include, with a few inches to spare on either side, the inner and outer edges of the wall foot. The measurement of the cut was 4 foot by 10 foot, and was intended to be as economical of labour as possible as the only digger was the owner. I was able to do the lighter scraping work but the doctors had recently stopped me doing the heavy digging, much to my annoyance and frustration on occasions like this!

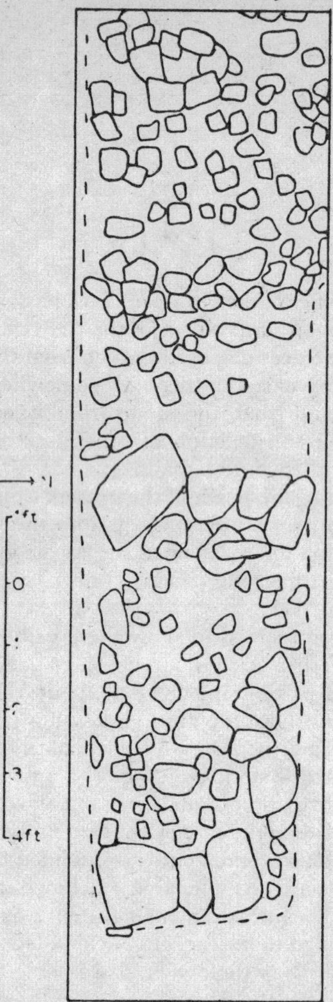

Fig 25. The House of Daviot. Part of the original Cut 1 showing stonework we uncovered.

At about 8 inches below the grass we came down on heavy stone work and the inner and outer edge of it is clearly marked, fitting nicely into our cut. As this first 10 foot length was successful we extended the cut further to the west and found more stone work. There was some mortar lying at the level of the bottom of the larger stones. The proper examination of this wall foot remains to be done as we had time only to excavate to the level of the bottom of the larger stones.

Later in the year we tried another cut across what appeared, from the dowsing, to be the western edge of this possible building site. This cut was also successful and produced the same type of stone work as did the original cut.

Much of the top of the area investigated by dowsing seems to be sand and, as I have mentioned elsewhere, I do sometimes find sand difficult and misleading to dowse over, but subject to this possibility for error I think the site is an interesting one and much information should be available by excavation.

Note. The ability by dowsing to place cuts accurately over objects to be examined.

CASE 14.

Field Drains.

A friend of mine was a dowser but did not practice much. Her son bought a small hill farm and found that the field drains in one field were blocked and the field in consequence was in bad condition. No one knew the exact position of the drains so to save a laborious search for them he asked his mother to find them by dowsing. She tried and failed.

Some days later she happened to meet me and told me the story. I asked her what she had been looking for and what question was in her mind. She said she had been looking for the water in the drains. So I suggested that as the drains were blocked there would not be running water in them and urged her to try again by looking for the field drains themselves. Later she let me know that she had done this and had been successful.

Notes. It is essential to get the question correct, clear and appropriate.

Practice and experience are desirable in each field a dowser works in otherwise avoidable mistakes like this will occur.

CASE 15.

Metal in a Man's Body.

When I was a very 'young' dowser I had spent half an hour telling a group of eminent professional archaeologists in Edinburgh that they ought to use dowsing means to assist them in their work. Of course I had got nowhere!

As I was about to go one of them asked if a dowser could find a piece of metal in a man's body. I replied that he should be able to do so if he was trained in that sort of work and I implied that I was not.

He promptly took off his jacket and laid himself on a table and challenged me to find a piece of metal that he said he had had in his back since the first World War.

I was horrified as I had never done anything like that before, but with five grinning faces looking at me I had no alternative but to try. So I got going and in about three seconds I had put my finger on a part of his back and he said 'By God you've got it!'

Notes. Have confidence that you can do it.

Be bold. Sometimes you have to take a risk and do what you have not done before.

Never guess, that is using the brain, but hand over to the Mind and let that feel out for the answer.

Learn to be oblivious to onlookers so that the mind can work without interference.

CASE 16.

Alluvial Tin.

In 1971 I went to stay with a professional geologist whom I did not know. As I got there he left to go to a meeting, but he told me that there was a bed of Alluvial Tin in the field just outside his garden and perhaps I would like to try my hand at finding and outlining it.

I was new to mineral dowsing at that time and had never seen Alluvial Tin before nor had I ever dowsed for it.

I went to the field and found by ground dowsing, what I thought was the outer edge of the bed and had it all marked out in about 30 minutes.

When he returned we went and looked at my markings and he said that I was correct. He knew where the outer edge lay because he had pitted across the field to establish the outer edge some time before.

Notes. No need for a sample.

Be prepared to take on new things, but be very careful and later learn the background of the type of work before doing much work in it.

Note the saving in time by dowsing. My work took 30 minutes and time must be allowed for the digging to prove my work, but this is very much less than the time taken to dig pits across the field systematically.

CASE 17.

Dating a Site in Caithness.

In 1972 I was searching Caithness by map dowsing for a very ancient type of archaeological site which I thought might exist there. Map dowsing seemed to show that such a site might exist in one place and it dated at between BC 7000 and BC 8000, so I made arrangements to visit the area so that I could confirm by ground dowsing and later by excavation that the site existed.

We had quite a treck to get there as it was right up in the hills. When we got there the ground dowsing confirmed the picture I had got by map dowsing but unfortunately there was no chance of confirming by digging then, because there was three feet of peat overlying the site and this I had not expected.

However there was a small stream running across the site which had cut a channel through the peat so I was able to cut back the peat bank beside the stream, cleanly, and take a sample from the very bottom of the peat. This sample I sent to the Macauly Institute in Aberdeen who very kindly tested it for me and dated the sample at about BC 7000. This was a very satisfactory date for me because any ancient archaeological site in the ground under the peat must date prior to the arrival of the peat and therefore must be older than BC 7000.

Here for the moment the situation remains.

CASE 18.

Following by Ground Dowsing.

This is a simple little story and is only included to encourage the novice. When I was starting dowsing I made a point of trying out all the things that the books claimed could be done by dowsing means.

The first time that I tried to follow a person was when my dog was being taken for a walk one afternoon and after they had gone I decided to try to follow the route they had taken, having no idea where they had gone.

I knew they had started out by the drive so at the end of the drive I tried with my rod to see which way they had gone and found that they seemed to have turned right and gone along the road, so I followed. Every 50 yards or so I checked to see if they had passed along this bit of road. After about 200 yards I came to a place where there was a turning into a wood which was a possible way they could have gone and here I checked again and found that they had turned into the wood and gone along the path which led through it. I continued along the path still checking periodically, for another 200 yards when I met them coming back. It was confirmed that my route finding had been correct.

I then suggested that they went on again any way they liked, but made it more difficult for me by making changes in direction. They set off and were out of sight in a short while so I gave them 10 minutes start and began to follow. I followed their line till I got to the end of the wood and here I found they had crossed over the fence and gone across a field, then at the other side of the field had turned sharply left up the hill along the fence. Some way later they had turned right over the fence into an area of trees and high bushes. I followed and found them sitting, hiding from me, behind the building in which fruit was stored. They confirmed that my idea of the route that they had taken was correct

By now I was very confident of my ability! It is said that 'Pride goes before a Fall' and this is particularly true in dowsing where over-confidence often leads to slipshod work and failure.

I asked them to go back to the house by any path they liked. From that spot there was a choice of about five possible paths all of which wound through fairly thick trees and bushes. I gave them a good start, then began to follow the 'scent'. Shortly I came to a place where the path forked and I had a choice between going right or left. I swung my rod to find which path had been used and picked up a scent on the left one which I followed. Eventually I arrived at the house confident that I had followed their route. In fact I had not. At the fork that I had tested they had turned right and I had got it wrong! In fact the fork had been used earlier in the day and had I tested both paths properly I might have got a better answer, but I had been slipshod and only tested the left one. This is quite a useful example of remenance which has to be kept in mind in this sort of work and allowed for.

Notes. Try out new applications of dowsing if they interest you or if they could be of practical use to you.

Confidence is essential but don't get brash, if you do so you will tend to fail.

Take trouble with your work, it pays always.